Before You Say I Do

Nuri Muhammad

NURI MUHAMMAD

ISBN-13: 978-1530258178
ISBN-10: 1530258170
Before You Say I Do. Copyright © 2016 by Nuri Muhammad.
All rights reserved. No part of this book may be used or reproduced in any manner whatsoever without written permission except in the case of brief quotations.
Printed in the United States of America. Published by Bashirah House Publishing - First Edition, 2016
Editing / Proofreading: Traci C. Muhammad (Phoenix, AZ)
Transcription: Deborah Muhammad (Columbus, OH) & Angela V. Muhammad (Houston, TX)
Cover/Interior/Editing: Rodney 'Asaad' Muhammad (Phoenix, AZ)
Cover Art Design: Jahleel Muhammad (Detroit, MI)

NURI MUHAMMAD

"Surely the men who submit and the women who submit, and the believing men and the believing women, and the obeying men and the obeying women, and the truthful men and the truthful women, and the patient men and the patient women, and the humble men and the humble women, and the charitable men and the charitable women, and the fasting men and the fasting women, and the men who guard their chastity and the women who guard, and the men who remember Allah much and women who remember — Allah has prepared for them forgiveness and a mighty reward."

Surah (The Allies) 33:35
Muhammad Ali Translation

Table Of Contents

Introduction	1
A Saving Grace	3
Temporary vs Permanent	5
Deposits and Withdrawals	9
Licenses and Learners Permits	15
Generational Dysfunction	19
Three Sides of 'Why'	21
The Top 8 Reasons To Never Enter A Relationship	25
Reason 1	25
Reason 2	25
Reason 3	26
Reason 4	27
Reason 5	28
Reason 6	28
Reason 7	29
Reason 8	30
The White Man's Formula	31
The Courtship Process	33
Fourteen Questions and Answers	35
~Question One~	35
~Question Two~	35
~Question Three~	36
~Question Four~	37
~Question Five~	38

~Question Six~	38
~Question Seven~	39
~Question Eight~	40
~Question Nine~	40
~Question Ten~	41
~Question Eleven~	41
~Question Twelve~	42
~Question Thirteen~	43
~Question Fourteen~	44
Love and Law	45
Instincts vs Free Will	47
Civilizing the Uncivilized	53
The Place and Role of Wisdom	59
The Restrictive Law Is Our Success	61
The Offer of High Civilization	62
Changing Our Mindset	65
Jesus and Divorce	67
Moses (Musa) Lifts Up A Serpent	69
Accepted Vs. Original	73
The Essential Ingredients	75
Ingredient One	75
Ingredient Two	76
The Originator	79
The Characteristics of a Real Man	83
The Second-Self	87
Epilogue	93

Direct Words of Guidance From The Honorable Minister Louis Farrakhan   **95**

INDEX   **105**

About The Author   **113**

Concordance of Scriptures   **115**

NURI MUHAMMAD

Introduction

The ultimate powerbase of the black man and woman is the family. In family we learn our past and define our future and occasionally because of family we redefine our future. The rise of the Black man and woman will be a direct reflection of the elevation of the family. Our families nurture us and are the lens through which we first view the world.

The initial establishment of a relationship creates a dynamic ripple effect that can either negatively or positively impact the soul of the person for generations to come. The Honorable Minister Louis Farrakhan once said, "they breed horses better than they breed people" meaning that more care and consideration goes into preserving and extending the blood line of thorough-bred horses than goes into perfecting and evolving the human being.

When Allah (God) is the true center of the relationship, then god's come forward and progress is unlimited, but when Allah (God) is an afterthought, then the progress of the couple is limited, stymied and erratic at best. In his first book, Bro. Nuri Muhammad wants to create a paradigm shift, wherein the reader will evolve to see family as the perfect reflection of the first Allah's self-creation and that family formation in this critical time must be seen as the foundation of dynasties. We are not only living in the now, we are creating the future through our words, deeds and actions.

That which is done out of sync with the time is done in vain and is born from a reptilian mindset. The entire existence of reptiles can be categories as a struggle to ensure three primary and primal needs—food, procreation (sex) and the seeking of shelter from the elements. For far too many people these same primal needs have become the motivating foundation for entering into relationships. We can no longer as a people afford to think only in terms of the *now*, we must think in terms of the *future perfect tense*.

Before You Say 'I Do' is the distillation of countless hours of, counselling combined with practical application into a single book designed to encourage not just lip-profession, but the practical application of a precise mathematical formula for the formation of relationships not based on this world's concepts of 'dating' but in accordance with the Divine Laws and commandments of God. In this book, the reader will learn the difference between dating and courting and the effect of each 'mind-set' on the formation of relationships.

Ultimately, the reader will be challenged to determine, for themselves, if they are forming a relationship for the *now* or establishing a *righteous dynasty for the future*.

Traci C. Muhammad
February 1, 2016

> "Allah is the light of the heavens and the earth. A likeness of His light is as a pillar on which is a lamp — the lamp is in a glass, the glass is as it were a brightly shining star — lit from a blessed olive-tree, neither eastern nor western, the oil whereof gives light, though fire touch it not — light upon light. Allah guides to His light whom He pleases. And Allah sets forth parables for men, and Allah is Knower of all things."
>
> —Holy Qur'an, Surah 24 (Al-Nur): 35

A Saving Grace

𝒥n the Most Holy name of Allah, The Beneficent The Most Merciful of those who have mercy. I forever thank almighty Allah (God) for doing something for us that He has never done for a people that have fallen from power and success the way the Blackman and woman of North America have fallen. Normally, when a people fall from power and success, God raises a messenger, a warner or a prophet but I thank Allah that He recognized the hell that we had caught under our 400 year old open enemy was so great and grievous that He would have to come and seek and save us, *Himself*.

I bear witness that the manifestation of this great intervention came to us in person, in the form of a well-made man named Master Fard Muhammad. I thank Allah for His coming and I know that I would not be speaking of the coming of such a great Saviour, a Saviour who traveled 9,000 miles, all by Himself, leaving behind paradise, to come into the hells of the wilderness of North America to save a people that were in hell, and I would know nothing of this Man, Fard were it not for a Georgia born Blackman by the name of The Most Honorable Elijah Muhammad.

I truly thank Allah for The Most Honorable Elijah Muhammad, he is the best friend that the Blackman and woman have ever had and if the white power elite were not so proud and arrogant, he would be the best friend they have ever had also. Why? Because it will be only by listening to him and following his blueprint for salvation that America could in fact be saved. I would never in this day and time be talking about these two were it not for one very special man walking amongst us today. He is the man that God has absolutely *anointed* and *appointed* for this dispensation of time in which we live today. He is our intervener *from* God, our teacher *from* God and our example *from* God. He is the developed model of what an ideal human being should be— he is the Honorable Minister Louis Farrakhan. It is in their names that I greet you the reader in these words of peace and paradise, in our original language of Arabic 'As-Salaam Alaikum' which simply means 'Peace be unto you.' This is the same greeting that Jesus greeted his disciples with and all those he met with and it is in fact a prayer, a prayer for peace.

Temporary vs Permanent

If you walk through any bookstore or do a quick search on the internet one thing will become very clear, the proper way to form a relationship is a topic that is critical to many. The word marriage alone, when searched on Google produced 677,000,000 hits. The question we must ask ourselves is if so many want to say 'I do', why do they end up saying after only a few days 'I don't?'

It seems as though anytime a person wants to take on this topic, that the initial response is overwhelmingly positive. Positive in the sense that we desire to hear the truth because we recognize that we have a problem with forming and sustaining lasting marriages and we are desirous of solving our problems, but negative, in the sense that it's such a big issue among our people— male and female relationships, that it has become the unfortunate hottest topic among black people, both young and old.

Choosing the right mate is the greatest decision that any human being could ever make, after picking salvation or religion? Our individual relationship with God is what is known as our primary relationship. Our relationship with the Supreme Being is the most important relationship above and beyond all relationships. Our relationship with Allah (God) stands apart. When we run the math and look at our connection to our children, our connection to our brothers and sisters, aunts and uncles, our connection to our spouses and even to our own mother and father. When we compare the human connections of family to the divine connection of Allah (God), all of these relationships are ***temporary***; however, our relationship with and to Allah (God) is the only ***permanent*** relationship we will ever have in our own life and that should tell us that if my relationship with my wife is temporary but my relationship with God is permanent then mathematically, God is infinitely more important than my wife. That should tell me if my relationship with my mother is temporary but my relationship with God is permanent then God is more important than my own momma. There is no other thing in existence that has a permanent tie to us but Allah (God), the Supreme Being. In fact, we had a relationship with Allah (God) **before** we even knew how to relate.

This is how powerful the relationship to Allah (God) is. What I want us to understand is that not only have we had a pre-existing relationship with God since before we were born. Not only do we have a relationship with God until we die but even after we're dead our relationship with God continues. The Holy Qur'an informs us that when one dies Allah (God) "takes the soul" and returns it back to its source. Well, the source of the essence or quintessence of our being, our soul, is the Creator Himself. He is without equal, without rival. So, all of us, without exception are operating on borrowed power from the God; and whenever we die, we return back to The One who made the deposit of life into our soul. This is why the Honorable Elijah Muhammad taught us that we should not morn and cry at funerals. We should not be so ignorant in our arrogance and boast that "ain't no funeral like a negro funeral." The reality is that in every Black family, everybody got a uncle, auntie, cousin or someone that will wait all the way to the end when they start 'cranking' it down and are about to die, to make a huge show and spectacle of things by going to the funeral and laying all over the casket, running around the church and falling out during the service. Then later on we find out that this 'loving and concerned' auntie only met the nephew twice and just barely knew him at all. She really just wanted to get some attention, but Allah says to us in Bible and Holy Qur'an that when He creates us He deposits in us of His own essence. Look closely at the terminology 'deposited.' Have you ever made a large deposit in a bank? The bank received the money gladly. So gladly in fact you didn't even need to show ID. "I'd like to deposit $20,000.00 into account number 68695432. 'Thank you sir and here's your receipt.' " When you come back to the same bank at the end of the week it's a whole different conversation then.

Deposits and Withdrawals

The conversation changes into something similar to this, "Yes, I'd like to make an eighteen thousand dollar withdrawal from my account. I put twenty thousand into it on Monday. 'Ok yes, please hold on a moment sir. Please have a seat right over here while I get the bank manager.' " Then they take you from the lobby back into the booth. Manger comes to you and says, 'Sir, why are you taking your money out? Have you ever thought about an IRA? Have you ever thought about a Mutual Fund? Have you ever…Have you ever….Is there something wrong? We have another savings format that will give you a one point five percent interest rate." See, whenever you make a deposit everybody loves you. What we must realize is that the bank is making a profit off the deposit that has been made. The bank is gaining interest off of you. They are actually taking your money and putting it into service for their personal benefit, not yours. The conversation completely changes when you go to make the withdrawal, now all of a sudden the bank teller, the bank manager they don't want to give you what you put into the bank. It shouldn't be our desire to be like a bank teller or a bank manager because if God made the deposit, He's got the right to make the withdrawal whenever He pleases.

Allah (God) tells us in the book of Jeremiah (1:5), "I knew you before you were born. I knew you in the womb of your mother. And then I formed you in the womb." Meaning, before we were born we already had a preexisting spiritual relationship with Allah (God) before we came into this dimension. Therefore, if Allah (God) is present during birth at death, after death and before birth, there is no relationship on the planet that trumps the relationship we have with Allah (God) the Supreme Being, the Creator of the heavens and the Earth, the Maker and Creator of all of us.

So, second to salvation, second to our relationship with God, is the bond, or the choice of a man or woman, to spend our lives and life energy with and on. Now what's so crazy is that in this world some of us are so needy that we settle for just anybody out of biological need and financial straightness. What we need to realize is that as a general rule, men choose women not because of love or the want or need to form an alliance (partnership) with a feminine counterpart that can help him become one with Allah (God), or for the purposes of discovering and fulfilling their purpose for living (existence). That's the right way to choose a mate, it's scientific, and it's mathematical. Far too often when a man is choosing a woman as a mate, as a wife, he's looking for a 'pleasure box,' a maid and a personal chef. When a man really chooses a mate for the right reasons, he chooses her as his feminine counterpart so that he can cultivate an alliance with the one who will help him grow into perfect union (oneness) with God and fulfill their collective purpose for living. Most men do not choose for purpose and oneness with Allah, they choose a woman because they are looking for pleasure.

A woman should carefully watch brothers in the sense that she examines their actions to discern their true motives. It is just as important for a woman to choose a man with whom she can create and sustain a mutually beneficial alliance with. The man should represent the spiritual and masculine side of nature who will and who can help you as a woman in the cultivation of your gifts, skills and talents in order for you to become one with Allah (God) and in so doing discover and fulfill your purpose for living. Sisters too often out of neediness choose a man that they are in truth looking to as a human ATM machine, a body guard, a surrogate father and a handy man.

Don't misunderstand me; a man's money is important. Don't believe me, think with me sisters; did you drink coffee this morning? Turn on the lights in your place of abode; walk outside to your car? A man's money is important and his ability to be courageous in order to protect and guard his family is important. No real woman wants a punk man! A man's ability to do things, repair, build and fix is very important also. Dear brother's it's important that a woman knows how to console you in matters that are mental, spiritual, and yes, in the physical way. It is also just as important that a woman is clean and neat—in her person, with her children and in her home. This is very important and since Black people have a saying that 'you are what you eat.' In reality, you are what you *ate* because it takes 24 hours for the digestion of food to be completed. So whatever we put in our stomach on Sunday we won't *'become'* that until Monday or Tuesday and at the end of the day, if you are what you ate then the woman that cooks for you is involved in the building of the new body that you will use to achieve your mission and objectives in life. Brother's don't you want a woman who can cook? That's important! But in this world the white man doesn't care anything about the health of the Black family!

In fact, when you study the history of Blacks and whites you'll find white people have always been attackers and destroyers of Black family life. Do you know why they are like this? It's because when they invaded Africa and began to look at the Metu-Neter, or the hieroglyphics on the walls of the pyramids, what the scientists saw were wall to wall images depicting proper and positive male and female relationships, fathers, sons, mothers, daughters and families. What we were telling the world is that family life is the *power base of **all** life*. When the military leader, Napoleon, went invaded Africa, his aim in part was to destroy all positive images of blacks with his primary objective being to seek out and destroy all of the original pictures of the *Black Jesus*. I said the original pictures. These new images of Jesus are not the originals; Michelangelo used his cousin as the model for all of his pictures, including Jesus. Michelangelo used his mother as the model for Mary. Napoleon's goal was to destroy **all** Black messengers, prophets, and angels but in the course of his journey, Napoleon saw on the pyramid walls these images of solid, strong Black family life. When he realized that Osiris the man was seated next to the images of Isis, his wife he was upset. When he saw on the pyramid walls an Egyptian god who was always pictured sitting right next to his wife. Notice closely, I didn't say girlfriend. I said his wife. This is a critical point that I want us all to understand.

No matter how closely you read the Bible and the Holy Qur'an you will never find the word 'boyfriend' or 'girlfriend' mentioned in either book. If boyfriend and girlfriend are not there in any scripture, then these are terms that are not in the language of God. These are man-made terms that come from a wicked mind-set that invented them to purposely subvert the power base of all Black life—*family*. When Napoleon looked he saw Isis in every image and the man right next to Isis. Why? Because not *behind* every strong man, but right *beside* every strong man is a strong woman. So when you go and look at these images of Osiris and Amon and others you'll see damage has been done. The damage was done because Napoleon ordered his men to use cannons to blow away the female who was always next to the man. And as a result of his actions, later on down the line of time, we in this modern time would not understand that for a real man to be his full self he has to have a good woman and before a real woman can be her full self she has to have a good man. Male and female are created to be interdependent entities that enhance one another.

Our former slave master's never wanted us to identify the basis of our real power. In order to hide this truth from us throughout time down to today, you can obtain a marriage license easier than a driver's license. You can get married easier than you can buy a used car. If you want to buy a house, hell, if you just want to get a cell phone plan, they will put you through more than the government will, if you want to get married.

Licenses and Learners Permits

In order to get married, all that is required is that you go downtown to the courthouse and show them some legal proof that you are 18 years of age or older and give them $18.00, which means that you can be in and out faster than at a fast-food restaurant. When you want to get a new cell phone they run your credit, which means they look back over a seven year period of your relationships with money and lenders. Then they demand three references and sometimes they will actually get on the phone and call whoever you put down as a reference. You may have a 750 credit score but they will tell you that you need more. Do you realize that before they will give you a driver's license you have to get a permit to learn how to drive but in order to get the permit to just learn how to drive you have to read and study? Why? Because you must acquire the knowledge of everything you may possibly run into while you're making your journey to and fro in the automobile for your safety and the safety of others who are also driving. After you go through all this you still don't actually have a driver's license. When you take your actual driving test, you are allowed to miss in most cases only two questions. If you miss more than what is allowed, not only do they not let you get a license, you can't even get a permit to even try to get a license.

When you pass the test, then you receive what is known as a learner's permit which simply means you must be chaperoned. To be chaperoned means that at all times somebody that knows how to drive and has already obtained an actual license has to be with you while you are learning how to drive. After all this when you take your test again, you are required to have logged in at least 40 hours of experience under the supervised view of a licensed driver. After all of this they still take you out on a road test in order for you to demonstrate what you have actually learned. Why, because in truth they don't actually trust you word that you were chaperoned and they point blank don't care what the paper-work says. 'Yeah you passed the written test but hell, prove to me that you can actually drive.'

Now brothers and sisters, don't you think that's a lot of steps to take just to get a driver's license? But what's so sad, is that when it comes to getting a marriage license, it's a little of nothing. We erroneously think that all we need to get a marriage license is to have some sort of warm and fuzzy feeling. A fuzzy feeling that tells us "I don't know what it was but as soon as I laid eyes on her… as soon as I seen him, I just knew he/she was the one." Six months later and you haven't finished paying for the wedding you couldn't afford in the first place and now you're in divorce court. Anytime you have a government that cares more about a driver's license than a marriage license what they are really outright telling us is that we care more about your ability to successfully navigate a vehicle on the road than we do about your ability to successfully navigate your life. What we need to understand is that it's up to us to care and take responsibility for our own lives and value them more than we value driving a car.

Now, let's examine this from a different angle. When it comes to driving and getting a driver's license the Department of Motor Vehicles (DMV) doesn't care if you have some warm fuzzy feeling about a car. No, they require that you demonstrate your level of responsibility regarding the car and those you will encounter while driving. So the DMV makes you read the rules, regulations and laws governing your ability to drive. They make you study so you can prove you have the requisite cognitive ability to comprehend all the things you may encounter while you're on the road going to and fro in your car. Question, what would happen if we thought like the DMV before we got married? What would happened if we had to read, we had to study, we had to learn the ins-and-outs of everything we could possibly run into in life before we ever could even get our permit and after we got the permit we had to be chaperoned and successfully go through forty hours of training? Then take a test with an agent, aka the father of the woman you want to take on as a wife? Yes, the reality is that a lot of father's aren't there. Well then what about taking the test with momma or grandma or grandpa? So now you've received a permit and 'you want to marry my daughter? Well let me take you out here for a little while so you can show me you know how to drive. Show me you know what it means to be a man. Show me you know what the purpose of marriage is.' Sisters you see the Brother want to ride in the car but he doesn't want to talk to your agent, who has your best interest at heart and is checking any potential driver to see if he has any outstanding tickets or warrants? Sister's does that make sense?

Brothers and Sisters, did you know that the divorce rate for Black people in America is higher than anywhere else on the planet? Is that an accurate expression of love? Love is not enough of a basis to say I do on. Let me make this clear, love is not enough of a basis to say I do. There has to be some knowledge present. We spend a whole lot of time making weddings "something to remember." We will flip through fifty different magazines looking for color schemes and ideas to create the perfect 'fantasy wedding'. Employ all sorts of strategic planning and budgeting techniques. Start dieting and create blueprints detailing everything from beginning to end. 'This is the song! No, no, no, start it right there at the second verse so it can coordinate with me entering through the door precisely.' All that energy put into a wedding; however, a wedding is a **day**, but marriage is for a **lifetime**.

Wouldn't it make more sense that we would study and plan more for the marriage than we study and plan for the wedding? In the Bible, the book of Hosea 4:6, it reads, "My people are destroyed from a lack of love?" No it doesn't say that it says, "My people are destroyed for a lack of knowledge." It's interesting when you realize that we never like to complete this verse, but the end of the verse says "because you have rejected knowledge." The Most Honorable Elijah Muhammad said every solution, to every problem, is found in a book somewhere. What this means is that the answers to all questions are already in the world. When we reject the library card, even though it's free, we reject coming to meetings, seminars, listening to lectures even though almost all of them are free, and because we have rejected knowledge scripture says, "I too shall now reject your children." This means that ignorance is in fact generational. Our marriages are destroyed from a lack of knowledge because we rejected knowledge and since we rejected knowledge God says in response, "I shall reject your children." Meaning, my ignorance is generational so I didn't know what I was doing in a relationship and I passed on my ignorance to my sons and daughters. Passing on to multiple generations this level of ignorance instead of passing on what God has already said.

BEFORE YOU SAY I DO

Generational Dysfunction

Most of us are familiar with the language "generational curse" if we grew up in a church environment and many of us out of ignorance, literally dismiss all known reason to make the illogical - logical as an excuse for our failure to comprehend the law of cause and effect. What kind of God would God be to condemn us based on our daddy, momma or grandmothers behavior? That's unjust. How can you hold someone 100% accountable for the mistakes made by a generation of people who preceded me that I have never even met? Mathematically speaking, we are at the most, twenty percent the product of our genetics with the other 80% being self-derived and measured based on our decisions—the law of cause and effect. Some genetic scientists argue that we are in fact composed of as little as five percent genetics and 95% choice. This is why we cannot sustain our lives because we are eating fast-food and taking in all manner of impurities in our bodies, and then we justify our actions by saying that "sugar (diabetes), high blood pressure and hypertension just runs in my family." The real question is if it runs in the family what kind of race is genetics running? Genetics is running a relay race.

In a relay race you have a baton that you pass on to the next person in the leg of the race. In the genetic relay race, great grandma, while she was running she passed it on to her daughter and her daughter took on the same bad habits as great grandmamma and integrated them into her lifestyle and the genetics relay race continues. Next thing you know your daddy got diabetes, high blood pressure and hypertension because he took everything his mama taught him and integrated it into his life and now in the genetic relay race he has the same habits that big mama had that grandmamma gave her and she gave to him. Next thing you know, here you are and you see your daddy and you running right beside each other and as soon as he hands you those same bad habits you grab the baton and keep on running. Understand this, we each have the power to break the generational curse(s) and completely heal. All we have to do is refuse to accept the baton of diabetes, hypertension, high blood pressure and it's all finished. Declare that from this day forward, we as a family are making new strides in a race. In this family I'm passing on the baton of optimal health to the next generation. Doesn't it make more sense to pass on health than sickness, suffering and death in the form of poor health?

Three Sides of 'Why'

There are three sides to 'Before You Say I Do' and within the three sides is a recipe that keeps us from one day saying 'I don't.' In the Bible, (Matthew 19:7-8) Jesus is asked by his disciples about divorce and Jesus responds, I don't know anything about divorce, "...for it was not as such in the beginning." In other words, Jesus is saying divorce is not natural.

The real making of a marriage doesn't come from just setting the timer on the oven. If you want to make anything you have to have a recipe, the right ingredients, and if you have a recipe that has an ingredient list that you decide to ignore, if the recipe calls for flour you don't put corn meal into the cake mix, no you follow the recipe. The same holds true in a marriage or you will complain, 'this marriage don't taste right.' Why because you ignored the fact that the recipe called for something specific but you said 'I'm still gonna bake the cake.' The three core points in this subject matter "Before you say I do" is first, what is your motive for getting married. Second, the procedure to say 'I do' and then third, the ingredients that go into making a lasting and successful marriage.

The Honorable Minister Louis Farrakhan said that when you want to know a thing you just ask *who, what, when, where,* or *how* about the thing. But when you want to *understand* a thing you must ask the question *why*? When you ask the question "why" it doesn't just allow you to judge the acts, it lets you judge the motives for the actions. You get into the motive by which someone does something that might even be looked upon as good, because you can have people doing a good thing for the wrong reason but it corrupts the good deed. Here it is a man walking an old lady across the street that looks like a good act but if the goal is to win her trust so that he can break into her house next week and rob her and kill her, that's a bad motive. The 'why', gives us the intent. The why, puts us at the core of the nucleus of an activity.

There are some reasons why someone should never start courting and absolutely should never get married. The right reason to start courting and to marry is to cultivate and obtain a spiritual alliance with the male or the female expression of God in the form of your mate in order to help them become one with God. To help the person achieve their purpose for living, that's why you start courting and ultimately marry. What is sad is that very few people come to the altar with this on their minds. One of the primary reasons why you should never rush into courting or marriage is because you are unhappily married at the present time. Picking a mate isn't like picking a car or negotiating a better lease or some deal. Picking a mate is in reality picking a life partner, a car is a transportation partner, but a mate is a partner to make you a God and bring children into the world to make the world a better place.

Now, the worst thing that we could ever do is when we begin to have problems in our present relationship, is to start talking to other people about the problems we are having, that's bad. But the worse thing is when you start talking to the opposite sex about your problems.

Understand, that there are different degrees in everything. You got good, better and then you got best and in the converse you got bad, wrong and worse. So bad can refer to talking to anyone. Wrong is talking to the opposite sex but you know what the worst is, talking to someone from the opposite sex that you were in a previous relationship with. Thanks to Facebook, all your ex's can find you and write on your timeline. In fact, your timeline is really a long list of past flings, past relationships; they're all there right on your timeline. If a man's with another woman but talking to you about his problems with her, that's not a good man. If a woman is with another man and she's telling you about problems with her man that's not a good woman because at a certain point whatever she ran into in him she will run into with you and she will go back down her Facebook list of friends and find another dude to do the same thing with.

The Top 8 Reasons To Never Enter A Relationship

Reason 1

Never enter into a new relationship because you are unhappily married at the present time.

Reason 2

Never start a relationship if you are separated. Separation is not the pre-requisite for divorce. The Honorable Minister Louis Farrakhan teaches us that separation is a time lapse inside of a relationship wherein which two people pull away from the physical, intimate, emotional responsibility of but this separation does not dissolve or absolve one from the financial responsibility to the marriage. You cannot say, "I ain't paying no bills! I don't live there no more. Ya'll the one who turned the heat up to 76 degrees. Hell you know if I was there it would be on 70 degrees and now ya'll done ran the bill all up, Ahhh hell naw!"

While separated, the financial obligations remain intact, what is not intact is the emotional and the physical aspects of the relationship. Separated and still sleeping together corrupts the process. Separation is a time to get your sanity back and carefully evaluate what you want out of the relationship and what you like and what you don't like about one another. After you obtain that information then you make a list and come back to the negotiation table to see if an agreement can be made to work on the identified list of things that really bother me and I can work on the few things that bother you and let's put our hands back together in the huddle and be a team again. This is what separation is for—it's a time to evaluate and renegotiate. Separation is not the time to start talking to other people. It's a time for you to talk to your God and yourself.

Reason 3

You should not get married if you are too immature. If you are a man and you love video games more than you like working, marriage is not for you. If you are a female and you love gossiping and shopping more than you like being a mother and a homemaker, then marriage is not for you. The Honorable Minister Louis Farrakhan teaches us that the mark of maturity that sets the stage for marriage is:

- you have to have lived on your own and prove you know how to pay bills,
- you can prove you know how to balance a check book and save money
- and you are self-sufficient

In other words, if you can't be a solid individual alone you can't build a solid marriage. You've got to prove that you know how to take care of yourself, before you ever start thinking about taking care of somebody else, let alone add children to this dynamic.

Reason 4

To make someone else jealous. This happens when you think 'She didn't want me so I'ma show her: I'm gonna find me a young girl, fine and dumb as hell, but she'll be fine with a well-rounded behind and a lop-sided mind.' Sisters stop worrying about getting 'butt injections' and focus on getting a 'mental injection' of the truth so you won't fall for the okie-doke coming from some smooth, talking brother. Entering into a relationship to make someone else jealous is not a proper motive.

Worse than entering into a relationship to make someone jealous, is when you are a member of a community, or a group of people, and you are aware that the person you are interested in is interested in someone else and you know that person is also interested in them, but instead of doing the proper thing, which is to step away and not interfere with the natural process, you decide to insert yourself in the process and corrupt it by making it seem suspect to each other, that's wicked. There are certain codes of ethics that we must abide by if we are to be honorable. If he's my brother, my friend, my partner and he's interested in her and I am too but he declares his interest first, it's wicked to move on her to make him jealous, this is a bad motive—a wicked motive.

Reason 5

To supply a person with self-esteem. When your self-esteem is so low that you cannot see anything good about yourself and you need someone in your life to tell you that 'you're so wonderful' constantly. Happiness is an inside job. *There is nothing you will ever find outside of you that will give you true happiness— it's an inside job.* Never should you invite someone into your life because you don't feel like you have any value alone because then you use the relationship to give you value which dooms it from the start. The Honorable Minister Louis Farrakhan teaches us in the *Self-Improvement: The Basis for Community Development, Study Guide* Number 11 that Allah (God) is the true center of **everything**, a relationship, or the lack thereof, is not the center. *Allah (God) is the true center of everything.*

Reason 6

When you are possessed of an irrational fear that your biological clock is ticking, this is how you form a relationship using a mathematical equation of absolute desperation. To form a relationship, under these conditions is to take, as they say in street terms, 'thirsty' to the next level. When you're thirsty you'll drink anything. When you're thirsty you just want something, you don't discriminate and will literally drink "anything." Whenever you begin to use age to justify desperation you end up settling for a peach *flavored* drink instead of a *real* peach drink.

Reason 7

When it will constitute what relationship experts define as a 'rebound relationship.' A rebound relationship is defined as one where you have just ended a relationship but to avoid looking into the mirror and engaging in deep and honest self-examination, self-analysis, self-correction and self-accountability for what your role was in the demise of the relationship, you rush and find somebody else to be with. Never should we enter into a relationship if we have not yet recovered from the disappointment, hurt or anger we experienced from the breakup of a relationship or a divorce or even the death of a spouse. It is a mathematical truth that two things cannot occupy the same space at the same time and likewise you cannot be married until you are truly single. Please understand, that just because you don't live with somebody, or have a court mate, doesn't necessarily mean that you are single.

To be single means that you have to be separated, at the heart of the connection, with whomever you were with, in the past. If you are fixated on what could have been or should have been you are not single. If you have not fully gotten over the past relationship, do not enter into a new one because what will absolutely happen is the first time you get into a disagreement the conversation will not be focused on how do we move past this but will go something similar to, 'You're not like Todd' and he will respond 'Hell you ain't like Laquesha' and how does she respond? With a 'Who is Laquesha?' and it's on from there but not in a good way.

Reason 8

Out of neediness. Sisters, never seek a man because you are tired of being a single mother and feel you need two incomes to maintain yourself and your children at a particular economic level or to reach a certain status. Sisters, you don't want a man just for an income. What happens when the money runs funny or even runs out? When one of you suddenly becomes unemployed? Has an injury that requires being off work for an extended period of time? Are forced to close your business? The stress of this as a constant threat to the relationship alone will cause the relationship to stay in a perpetual atmosphere of enmity and strife. If you have established a relationship just for income, for money, then know that you are in deep trouble.

Brothers can be needy, desperate and thirsty too. Brothers want to use the excuse that: 'I'ma real man, a natural man, and I find women attractive. Yeah, I understand the Restrictive Laws and all that, but I'm saying keeping it real, I'm a man and something gotta give. I got needs.' Brothers, discipline— *self-discipline produces self-mastery*. Brothers must make the conscious decision to think with the 'big head' instead of the 'little head.'

The White Man's Formula

Over the years we have tried the white man's formula for relationships, by sitting at home watching everyone from Dr. Oz, to Dr. Phil and some are so crazy and aberrated that they even watch Jerry Springer. These people don't know what they're talking about! They are in fact hypocrites because they need the very thing they are trying to convince you that you need. We tried to do it the way our parents and our grandparents did it and the general rule is our parents taught us to tolerate a whole lot of whatever in a relationship.

Almost all of us have grandfathers or uncles that have a whole different family we didn't know about till the child was 32 years old and showed up at the funeral. When you start doing the back track on the timeline you realize, the mother of the newly discovered child lived right around the corner from your auntie or my grandmother's house. You remember how you used to wonder why grandpa or uncle was always over there working on the roof. Then you question your Grandmamma 'Uh, did you know granddaddy had six children by Susie? You know Susie, who lives right around the corner from here?' Grandma over in the rocking chair crocheting, 'Yes baby, I *been* knowing that.' Now confusion sets in and the challenge is to rise above your emotions. Now you want to know why the whole family seemed content to keep this a secret? How did a whole human being that has the same father as you come into the world and you didn't even know they existed?

Learning, by necessity to cope with low standards from our brothers, sisters, mothers, fathers and our grandparents gave us de-facto permission to never seek to try and start a relationship according to the expressed way and Will of God.

I want to give you what The Most Honorable Elijah Muhammad, explains is the best way of starting a relationship. This is *Muhammad's Process*. Yes, we do have divorce in The Nation of Islam, but we do not have divorce nearly at the level, not just among blacks but even among whites in the Nation of Islam. White people have a 50% divorce rate in America, Black people have a 75% divorce rate but we in the Nation of Islam have a 20% divorce rate. With one of the main contributing factors, in our divorce rate being the fact that we consciously and purposely ignore the courtship rules. In the Nation of Islam, God gave a way, a manner, to The Honorable Elijah Muhammad, that even though all you need in this world is $18.00 and an ID to obtain a marriage license, in the Nation of Islam you have to go through something called the "courtship process."

The Courtship Process

Courtship is defined as an intentional process wherein two people, make a conscious decision to engage in discovery, to determine if they share enough compatibility and characteristics, in crucial areas, to get engaged and ultimately to marry. According to Webster's dictionary, the word courtship is defined as 'the act, process, or period of courting, or wooing.' To 'woo' means 'to try to get somebody to fall in love or to seek someone as a spouse, to cultivate.' The Honorable Minister Louis Farrakhan has taught us that when you look at the word courtship, the base word is 'court.' When a matter is brought before a legal court, the actual facts must be determined through the process of discovery in order for a decision or judgement to be made. In a trial, there is a process of discovery and in courtship there should also has to be the same process.

In courtship, the goal is to try to discover as much truth about the person as we can, in order to use this information in the process of determining if the two individuals are compatible or not for a successful, long-term marriage. Courting is not dating. Why? Because dating is playing around while courting is serious. What makes courting different from dating is that courtship is a process with a specific intention attendant to it. Meaning, the individuals in the courtship approach it with a mind-set of 'I'm looking for a wife or a husband' whereas dating is a process of discovery where individuals involved are seeking someone to play around with and possibly to marry at some point.

Dating might last for three months, three years, or it may be for a lifetime. That's dating, where you're 'playing relationship', 'playing house'.

The Honorable Minister Louis Farrakhan specifically answered thirteen of the following fourteen courtship related questions posed to assist attendees of the annual Nation of Islam's Singles Retreat in their quest to gain invaluable insight into a critical aspect of the Science of Mating. *His answers must be studied deeply because these answers given by the Honorable Minister Louis Farrakhan guide our minds to a clearer understanding of the purpose and direction of our own lives.

---

*Editor's Note: *The full questions posed to the Honorable Minister Farrakhan, along with his complete answers can be found at the conclusion of this book.*

Fourteen Questions and Answers

~Question One~

'Is it true that a man should marry someone half their age plus seven?'

While many of us saw the Malcolm X movie, this is not the teachings of The Most Honorable Elijah Muhammad. There is no set age for the choosing of a mate. "A young man can be with an older woman, an older man can be with a younger woman or you can find someone that is your exact age." Compatibility, according to the Honorable Minister Louis Farrakhan, has nothing to do with the amount of calendar years you have achieved but it has everything to do with the level of maturity that you possess.

~Question Two~

*What is the proper way of starting a courtship?**

When a brother sees a sister that he thinks will make him a good wife – **wife** not bed-mate but wife, he should mention this to the Student Minister, Student Captain or the Student Lieutenant to determine if she is available. A brother should never approach a sister to inquire about her marital status or state his interest in her prior to doing so. The proper procedure is to take the disposition that 'I see you, but I won't let you know that I see you'. Proper procedure sisters is if you might be interested, is that you do not add extra scoops to the dinner when the brother comes through the line, then everybody starts wondering and talking about 'damn, how come he always gets so much food?' What are the M.G.T. doing? No it's not *the* M.G.T. it's *that* M.G.T. that likes *that* F.O.I. That's how *that* F. O. I. got so much fluffed carrots on his plate right there. Before we leave this point, the Honorable Minister Louis Farrakhan also stated that, yes; it's permissible for a sister to ask for a brother in courtship. It's better for the man to be the initiator; however, if a sister sees a brother if she wants to, she can go through that same procedure and ask for the brother in courtship.

~Question Three~

'Is permission or approval needed to court someone? Do the student labors have the right to deny a courtship request?'*

The answer from the Honorable Minister Louis Farrakhan is: Emphatically no! No one's permission or approval is needed to court someone; however, out of courtesy one should inform the laborers that you are entering into a courtship and no official should deliberately block a believer from courtship. There is no laborer that has any authority over who a Believer chooses to court. If the laborer has concerns about someone, they should arrange to meet with the brother or sister and share their concerns but they should not meet with both of them together. Speak to them and provide your advice only. After the meeting, if they say, "yes sir, yes ma'am, thank you yes I'll take that information into consideration" that's the end of that conversation. Again, no laborer can block any courtship of any Believer.

We can encourage, we can give advice, but we cannot stop the process.

~Question Four~

How long should a brother be in the Mosque before he can ask for a sister?*

The Honorable Minister Louis Farrakhan says: "If a sister has been in the mosque for a significant amount of time and the brother is just coming in and he sees a sister it is better **not** to court. Let that brother get trained in the way of God, at least three to nine months." To take this point deeper, Sisters, let God make a man out of him before you try to make a husband out of him. Brothers, same thing applies to a sister who has not been in for a significant amount of time. Don't just get a sister and she just got registered. Nor should you go out and fish in a sister or brother and then use as your angle: 'If you get registered, I'll marry you.' No, your job is to fish them in from the sea of sin into the house of God, not into your personal house.

If a woman is coming to the mosque believing that if she gets 'registered' she will get a husband, then the process of pure motive has been corrupted. She doesn't join to join onto a percentage (or portion) of belief in Allah (God) and another percentage (or portion) of a belief in you, when this happens, as she gets to know you, her belief in you will go down and when it goes down, her faith could possibly go down with it.

You should desire and want a woman who is here because she believes in Allah (God) 100% and you become the extra icing on the cake.

~Question Five~

Should a courtship be announced to the believers?*

No, a courtship should not be announced. The engagement is a public affair and it should be announced, courtship should be made known to the laborers and to the family members.

~Question Six~

Does courtship include pre-marital sex?*

The Honorable Minister Louis Farrakhan teaches us absolutely not because as soon as sex is introduced into the courtship, the courtship is over. Sex has an influence on a person that is akin to becoming intoxicated. The intoxicating influence of sex on one's judgement causes their ability to be rational to become clouded, which in turn compromises and impairs your ability to make a sound and sober decision.

In courtship, there should be no kissing, no touching, rubbing or holding of hands. You should not even sit in the front seat with one another when you drive. This is for each person's **protection**. Courtship is not engagement, it is not marriage. You do not want to engage in any activity that could put you in a position which may potentially turn into a 'situation' wherein you end up getting caught up and caught out there. Deceptive intelligence will say, 'It's just a little peck on the check.' Understand that by nature we are emotional beings and we live in an over sexed society where one peck on the cheek causes many to jump up and down thinking they see cupid, hearts and fireworks. Bottom line: **Keep your hands to yourself!**

~Question Seven~

What is the Nation of Islam's view of an older sister and a younger brother in a courtship? How old should a person be before they start courting? Age 18?*

The Honorable Minister Louis Farrakhan says that it's not about reaching the age of majority because 18 years of age does not necessarily demarcate maturity. The Honorable Minister Louis Farrakhan said, "I know some 18 years olds that are ready to be married, but I also know some 48 year olds that are not. It's not about age, it's about maturity. There are decisions that must be made by people of mature thinking. Advice and council by wise and mature spiritual guides is necessary." If you are very young, and you have what they call puppy love, you want to get some people who have full grown love to sit down and talk to you, to help you understand the difference between love and lust. Help you discern if the feeling is real, an expression of genuinely divine interest or just an impure infatuation. If you really want a wife or if you want a girlfriend; a husband or a boyfriend and let them help you determine if you should move forward or if you should wait awhile longer before entering into courtship.

~Question Eight~

How long should I wait after a courtship has ended before going into another courtship?*

There is no time limit. It can be immediately. This is what the Honorable Minister Louis Farrakhan stated, "there should be some time" that goes by in order "to allow you to heal from the emotional strain of a breakup before entering into another courtship however; you should not have that much of an emotional attachment to someone if you haven't been touching on them."

~Question Nine~

If your court mate is placed in Class F, what happens to the courtship?*

The courtship ends and after 90 days you can resume the courtship; however, if someone has been put out for 1 to 5 years, meaning they are guilty of adultery or fornication, the courtship is over permanently. This's God's way.

~Question Ten~

What about confidentiality during courtship?*

You can ask any questions you want to ask during courtship as early as you want to ask them. Courtship is about discovery. According to the Honorable Minister Louis Farrakhan, you should ask the person, "Do you have a sexually transmitted disease. You can ask that from day one." You can ask *whatever* you want to ask just understand that you will get some 'what had happen was' responses, but if you can bust through the 'what had happen was' responses to arrive at the truth, then your final decision will be made based on actual facts.

Anything you want to ask you can ask but what you learn in a courtship about another brother or sister is confidential-forever. Never should the information learned be exposed to anyone. Not even the student laborers, unless what they are going to do or are doing is going to hurt or injure themselves or someone else.

~Question Eleven~

What are the roles of the chaperone?*

Earlier on when we analyzed the driving test and we concluded that you have to have somebody with you that knows how to drive to truthfully verify your 40 hours? Same rule applies in courtship. You must have a chaperone. This is done to keep those who are attracted to each other from entering into pre-marital sex which then stops the process of courtship. The role of the chaperone is to be the 'moral police' to guard them from not just fornication but from going near fornication. The act of kissing, holding hands, putting your arms around each other at the movie, all of this is going near fornication. Stay away from the whole area.

A chaperone should be given at least one weeks' notice when possible; you must be considerate of the chaperone's time. This is high civilization, not Negro relationships 101; this is the way you make kings and queens out of Black people. High civilization.

The courting brother should pay for **all** expenses, the person he's courting and the chaperones expenses. Brothers, when you can't pay for all the expenses be upfront and advise the chaperone in advance of the anticipated costs and confirm that they are willing and able to pay their own expenses.

~Question Twelve~

Is it proper to assist the person that you are courting with paying bills?*

The Honorable Minister Louis Farrakhan said "no." It is not proper to pay bills. It's not proper to give or to accept gifts during the courtship. The giving of personal and expensive gifts is discouraged because it sets up a precedence of expectation. You don't give gifts to the judge, if you give a gift to the judge and the judge accepts the gift, its considered bribery which then corrupts the judge's decision making process. In courtship, no gifts should be given or accepted because that's bribery.

~Question Thirteen~

At what point should you introduce your children to the person you are courting?*

The Honorable Minister Louis Farrakhan teaches that, "It's wiser to not introduce them in the initial stages of courting but when the parties are getting serious about each other and intend to be engaged, it is then that you offer another aspect of discovery, by bringing that person into a relationship with your children to see how they will mesh with your children. How the children will mesh with them because all of this should impact the decision for engagement and marriage." Additionally, he also teaches that "If you're a mother, with young children, and you're courting someone and arrive at the point where you're thinking about becoming engaged and you introduce them to the children and you take a month or so trying to help them get to know them and your children say I don't like him, **You cannot marry that man.** You are a package deal Black woman and never should you ever separate your bond with your sons or your daughters to please no nigger on the planet. Always look out for them as number one." The footnote to this is: If your daughter is 24 and your son is 30 and they come to you and say, 'Ahhh mama, I ain't digging him' your answer should be 'so what you're grown!' Whenever you're dealing with grown children they don't have a say. *The opinion of the little children is important however.*

~Question Fourteen~

How long should an engagement last?*

Courtship, the Honorable Minister Louis Farrakhan, says "there's no time period on courtship." He said, "however, long courtships are bad because the longer you court the more you began to bend and break rules. Did you ever hear grand mama say 'why buy the cow when you can get the milk for free?' There are certain things that you can't give to one another until you've proven, by contract, that you are with me for rest of my life. Then I'll give you what you're asking for but an engagement could be one month, three months, but no longer than six months.

Should an engagement take place and you for whatever reason can't get it together to have a wedding in six months you're not serious about getting married. It's not necessary to have a big expensive, extravagant wedding. It's better to have an inexpensive wedding and a beautiful expensive, extravagant marriage. We've been hustling backwards when it comes to courting, engagement and marriage.

Love and Law

We are eager to find a mate, to enter into courtship and marriage. Many search and search and sacrifice all sorts of things in order to experience "love" but what many fail to do is to really seek to understand what "love" really is and what it really means to love. When we enter into a deep, scientific study of **Love**, we find that there is in fact no limit, in terms of a definition for love. Love is an action word that requires our acceptance of the first phase of love, which is The **Law,** to be real and to be fully experienced.

If we have not experienced the joy of living according *to* the Law of God, from the outside looking in, being "law-less" looks more attractive than being "law-ful". Imagine riding down the street and going to the mall, you see two people (male and female) laughing—having what appears to be fun. They appear to be having so much fun while with one another, and then you look closely, at their hands, you notice they're not wearing wedding rings. When you see two other people, male and female and you see them both with wedding rings but they look to be very unhappy. This is when we realize that sometimes the worst advertisement for the institution of marriage is married couples themselves. Sometimes married couples make lawfulness look like it is slavery. While the lawless make lawlessness look like it is so much fun.

If one is judging and looking from the outside only, it does seem like the club-hopper is having more fun than the one who is striving to be upright. It seems like the one that smokes, drinks and does whatever they *feel* like doing is having more fun and experiencing more joy in life than the one that has voluntarily disciplined their life. Without the law of God being imposed from the outside in, by those that have decided to discipline themselves, then those that are not disciplined from the outside in will think that righteousness looks unattractive and too difficult. Their thought is sometimes, "I'd rather just do what I feel like doing whenever I feel like doing it." What they don't realize is that it is the proper application of "law" that ultimately leads us into the mind frame, wherein, we may truly love one another.

Unlike human's, animals cannot love. Dog lovers may fool themselves into thinking, "Oh, my dog loves me." No the dog doesn't, don't believe me, stop giving the dog water. Stop giving him "Kibbles and Bits". Stop petting him. Stop cleaning out the doghouse, stop letting him in the house when it's too hot or too cold. Start neglecting the dog that you think loves you and then you'll find out that the same dog that used to hug up next to you will be across the street on somebody else's porch and when you whistle, "Come here, Spike!" Spike won't respond because Spike is getting fed better, getting cleaner water, and getting a warmer place to sleep while you neglected him. That means the dog doesn't love. *The dog is loyal by means of fulfillment of a need.*

Instincts vs Free Will

Not only do animals not love, they do not need law. Animals have their law engrained in their nature. It's called **instinct**. In truth, it's wrong to kill the lion that ate the lamb. It's wrong to get mad at the bear for eating the cattle. It's wrong to go and hunt down the pack of wolves—in the woods—that got a hold of a few sheep on a ranch. The wolf, the lion and the bear didn't break the law. They don't have law—they have instinct. They know "kill or be killed". They know "prey or predator". And whenever the opportunity knocks and they find something that looks like it's weaker than them—intellectually based on an environmental understanding or physical strength, then they see themselves as predator and it as the prey. If an animal sees you with something that looks like it could harm them (fire, some object, a car, anything bigger in physical size than the animal itself) then they default to nature which demands either they're going to kill or be killed.

Instinctively, the animals are in accordance with the law of God 100% *all* of the time. When you have a tiger in the circus or the zoo, there is nothing wrong with the tiger; it's something wrong with trying to make the tiger jump through a ring of fire. When the lion wakes up and realizes "Wait a minute…this is that same man that as a cub tore me apart from my mother, beat me when I didn't do what I was commanded, and starved me when I did what was natural. Yet this same trainer has his head inside of *my* mouth." The lion, operating on instinct decides to close his mouth and the man loses his head; there's nothing wrong with the lion. It's something wrong with the man for sticking his head in the lion's mouth in the first place!

Man, human beings are different. Man does not have instinct. Man has been given something called "free will". Which means man can consciously choose right and wrong. Man has the authority of intellect to do what he pleases, even if what he pleases is against the Law of God and the Law of Nature. This is an example of how much Allah (God) respects the human being. When you study the mind of an animal—you realize that the animal never makes the excuse of "had I been in my *right* mind, I would not have done such and so." You'll never hear an animal, that's if they could talk—they would never say, "Had I listened to my *first mind*..." You'll never hear an animal say that, "If I'd just listened to that voice *within me,* that told me not to go there—not do that, then I would have avoided the conflict."

Animals do not have a "voice" of reason. Animals only possess a first mind. They do not have a second, a third or a fourth mind to which they could listen in order to regret not listening to the first one. Animals cannot say, "Had I only been in my *right* frame of mind..." Animals are **always** in their right frame of mind. But man has said—and does say, "If I had only listened to my first mind...If I had only been in my *right* mind; if I had just listened to that *first* voice inside of my head, then I never would have said, I never would have gone there, I never would have done that, I never would have spoken that, I never would have drank that, if I had just been in my *right* mind or listened to that *first* thought." If we *did* listen to the first thought, and we did something contrary, that means we had to listen to another thought. If we didn't act out of our *right* mind, then we had to act out of our *wrong* mind. This presupposes that man and woman have more than one mind.

We have one brain, one head but inside of this thing called

"mind," there are four different minds 'inside' of it and depending upon the *motives* for the choices we make, this will determine which version of 'mind' we are actually fed by the most. When Jesus says: *"As a man thinketh, in his…"* What?"… *heart so is he."* Well, if we have four minds inside of our mind, depending upon which one we utilize the most, this will determine what we **are**.

The highest mind is the mind of **God,** followed by the mind of *man*, then *beast*, with the lowest form of mind being the *reptilian mind*. Reptiles are only interested in food, sex and shelter. Beasts are only interested in appetite, lust and desire. Man thinks with logic, and reasoning, and God functions from supreme wisdom—and revelations. If we are making decisions based on what has been revealed if we are making decisions using Supreme Wisdom then we are making them with an understanding of the law of cause and effect knowing that what we **think** we will **become**. When we make our decisions out of wisdom, out of revelation, then we become "a god". If we make our choices and they are motivated by rational, logical, analytical thought, I'm a "human being". But if the reasoning I utilized to make the decision was based on appetite, lust, or sheer desire, then even though I am born a human being, scripture doesn't say, *"As a man is **born** so is he"* or *"As a woman is **born**, so is she"* — understand that even though we are born, and we walk on two legs, we drive cars, we cook, we bring children into the world, we raise them, we learn, we do all the things that human beings do, yet if my decisions are rooted in appetite, lust and desire, we become beast in human form. If we are making decisions just from a need for food, sex and shelter, then we are operating from the lowest level—and that's a reptilian level. A reptile doesn't have a backbone. Any time an object does not have a backbone, it is like a snake—a snake cannot move into an upright position unless it finds something to crawl up on that is *already* erect.

The Honorable Elijah Muhammad teaches us that even though the Caucasian has a spine, 4,000 years ago when they were sent into the hills and cave-sides of Europe they went savage. They lost the knowledge of self. They didn't know how to cook, how to build a home for themselves, how to rear their young, they even lost the ability to speak. Several years ago there was a movie called "Quest for Fire" the movie detailed the life of cave people. They weren't using "The King's English" to communicate in the movie— they were grunting. They were not walking upright—they were crawling around on all fours. The cave people had a spine, but because they went savage on the inside, in their thinking, then their bodies began to reflect their insides. Meaning, that since they had a bent over mentally they began to bend over physically.

Why is this important to understand, because you see so many Black men today walking with a limp to draw attention to themselves but what's the limp really about? Why are you limping Blackman? Logically, if you're limping, and the only time you should to be limping is when something is physically wrong with your leg, yet you're limping, it's not because something is wrong with the Black man's leg; it's because something is drastically wrong with his head (his thinking). After the Caucasian lost all his knowledge, he began crawling around on all fours, now the Blackman is walking around with a limp, then this means we are in a state of savagery where we too have lost the knowledge of *ourselves*. Just like the Caucasian, are living a beast life, so are Black men. We, too, don't know how to build a respectful home, how to rear our own children. Therefore, we are limping. Our legs are messed up because our heads are messed up.

"Moses" in Arabic is spelled "Musa. M -*u-s-a*". Letting you know that the *real* Moses wasn't 4,000 years ago in the caves dealing with White people, or in Egypt dealing with some Jews. The real Moses is in The United States of America (U-S-A) because we are "The Children of Israel". *Pharaoh* is the President. "Egypt" means "land of bondage" — that's America. Black people are the only people historically held in bondage for 400 years. Scripture doesn't say, "As Moses *freed* a pyramid builder, so shall the coming of The Son of Man be" — In the Bible it says, "As Moses lifted up a serpent, in the *wilderness*, so shall the Son of Man also be lifted up". (John 3:14) The Honorable Elijah Muhammad teaches us that this scripture is a real description of the work of Moses. Moses was not going to free a pyramid builder. The Moses of 4,000 years ago was a prophet to the White race. He went into the caves and hills of Europe to deal with human beings that didn't think like God. They didn't think like men, they didn't even think like beast. They thought like reptiles!

Civilizing the Uncivilized

When Moses found them, he had to teach them some of the forgotten tricknology that Yacub had taught them which was: lying, stealing, and how to Master the Original Man. He also had to teach them how to build a home (a respectful home) for themselves. If that was the state of Moses work, and the scripture says, "...as Moses lifted a serpent up in the wilderness, so shall the coming of The Son of Man be", then we, the Black man and Woman of America have met the Son of Man! Which means, that just as the Caucasian was in a *physical* state of savagery, living in a *physical* cave, and *physically* blind, which required a *physical* operation to correct, then so too are Black people in the same state, but on a psychological level.

In Surah 18 of The Holy Qur'an, entitled "The Cave" this surah is referring to a hole in the middle of a mountain. The Holy Qur'an says that this cave is the mark of Christianity. A cave, by definition, is a dark and damp environment. Anything that is in a dark and damp environment promotes the growth of disease. What has church been like for us? It's a very dark and damp environment. We haven't gotten *stronger* in Christianity—we have gotten weaker.

All the Caucasians caves were north facing. If the sun rises in the east and sets in the west, then those in the north never received direct sunlight. Scientifically/medically speaking, if you were placed inside of a dark closet for a day or two then when you come out you would have to re-gain your sight. They weren't in a closet—they were in a cave not for a day or two but for 2,000 years! So they were *completely* blind. We, too, have gone spiritually blind. As Moses lifted up a serpent in the wilderness, so did The Honorable Elijah Muhammad and so is

The Honorable Minister Louis Farrakhan lifting a people up in the wilderness of North America.

What did it take for Moses to erect and raise the Caucasian back to an upright level? It took THE LAW. So in the scriptures, *"Thou shall not steal"; "Thou shall not kill". "Thou shall worship no other God"; "Thou shall not make any graven images". Thou shall not lay down with thy own family members"*. These aren't human beings Moses's is talking to; he's talking to some savage reptilian freaks! Moses had to deal with them. In fact, even though Moses was giving them knowledge, they didn't like that he was *changing* them. The Honorable Elijah Muhammad teaches us that Moses had to sleep in the middle of a ring of fire. When Moses found the Caucasian crawling around, he had to put a board in their back. The Honorable Elijah Muhammad explained that Moses invented the girdle. Moses used to put a board on their back and then tie it up so that they couldn't bend back over and crawl—this forced them to stay erect. When you go from crawling to erect, they call that UP-Right. Just as a board and a girdle were used by the 4,000 year old Moses to get that savage upright, we now have been given The Restrictive Laws of Islam—which is the *spiritual board* in our back to get us upright.

The Honorable Minister Louis Farrakhan says that you don't need law if you're not law-less. Law only prescribes *the limits* that Allah (God), imposes on the human being for your growth, your development, and your success in the life that He gives you. When you grow, starting with law (starting with imposing limits on yourself) you grow into that out of which the law came—*you grow into love*. You grow *into* Allah (God), then there is no need for law because "love" is the essence of the law and there is no law greater than love. **Love** becomes the exterior prohibitions (or the prescribed limits) imposed from the outside in.

Whenever you grow out of law into love, you are no longer in need of someone on the *outside* imposing limits on you. When you have love, you become the imposer of limits from the *inside out*. When Jesus first met Matthew, Mark, Luke, John and the others—they became known as "The Disciples". Later, they were known as "The Apostles". But they were the same group of men, the name change denoted that they had just reached a different stage of spiritual development.

The base word of "disciple" is **discipline**. Meaning, when he first met them, he *disciplined* them from the *outside in*: "*Don't do that*", "*Go ye, not, unto the gentile people, nor by the way of the Samaritans—but go ye, only, to the lost sheep of the House of Israel*". (Matthew 10:5-6) He always had to tell them what *not to do* and *what to do*. But at a certain point, the same group of people did not wear the title "Disciple" they began to wear the title "Apostle". A "disciple" is one that is disciplined from the outside in, while an "apostle" is one who is disciplined from the inside out. A disciple **needs law**, but an apostle **has love**.

Law is the exterior prescribed limits and without the law, we would not have a standard to compare ourselves to. You say, 'I thought we were righteous by nature'—yes, but we're not living by nature. The law of motion says that a body at rest will remain at rest or in that condition or state unless it is acted upon by a superior exterior force. Then another aspect of the law of motion says that a body at rest will remain at rest and even if it is in motion, will continue in the direction it started in unless acted upon by some superior external force.

When the White man finished breaking us, he gave us the title "Negro". **Negro**, from the Latin "nigra", which means **dead**. Necrology is the study of the dead. Any time you look in the dictionary for the prefix "necro" it's always something dealing with *death*. If the slave master made us into "dead" — sleep objects — then we will remain in this condition unless and until we are acted upon by a superior exterior force. Law has to come; organization has to come; instructions have to come; rules, mandates, discipline has to come — and somebody has to *lead* us, *guide* us, *instruct* us, *reward* us, and *punish* us that we might grow back *into* love — which is our nature.

Why will a body at rest remain at rest, and why even if it is in motion will it continue to move in the same direction unless it is acted upon by another force? It's because even though a person might be alive, the brain has two primary goals by way of default. The brain's two primary goals are to *avoid pain* and *seek pleasure*. Nothing would be wrong with that *if* — pain were not the mother of growth and change. Nothing would be wrong with avoiding pain if *pain* wasn't weakness leaving the body. If pain is the mother of growth and change and it is weakness leaving the body — how will we ever grow, how will we ever change if we don't face some difficulty and endure some pain? The Honorable Minister Louis Farrakhan teaches us that there is a *difficulty factor* attached to everything of value.

If we listen to the default thinking of our minds, we will avoid everything that challenges us and stimulates growth and change. If we obey the default menu of our brain we'll seek pleasure — always. Drugs give you pleasure **now**...but pain later. Many things that are available in the world give pleasure, but not long term or lasting pleasure. The brain is geared to seek pleasure and avoid pain without restrictions—without laws, without rules and regulations; we would not have the guiding principles necessary to let us know where we can lawfully find ease, without violating the long term goals of life.

The Place and Role of Wisdom

As Muslim followers of the Divine Teachings of the Honorable Elijah Muhammad, we have been given, by Master Fard Muhammad, something called **The Supreme Wisdom**. In "The Original Rules of Instructions", Number 10, it opens with: *"The Restrictive Law of Islam is our success…"* What does this mean? It means that the *Restrictive Law* is our personal insurance policy against failure. If we stay in the bounds of The Law, we're going to find ourselves being successful. The minute we go outside of the Restrictive Law's then we lose our policy—our insurance lapses, and we wind up having an accident and we are unsuccessful. From the Lessons we learn that, *"Anyone who fails to be one hundred (100%) to The Law shall be dismissed from his or her post."*

Question: Honestly, how many of us have actually been 100% in accordance with The Law? The first Restrictive Law says, *"Obey Allah and His Messenger"*. *"Obedience to The Messenger is Obedience to Allah, as The Messenger is the bearer of Allah's message to you and I"*. Have we obeyed **everything** that The Messenger of Allah, the Honorable Elijah Muhammad has said? There's no point in examining the remaining laws when we are honest about this law. However, it's one thing to be absent from a post or position of leadership, but it's something totally different to be absent *in* a post or position. *Everybody* has leadership responsibilities. *Everybody* has a post. Understand that our successfulness in a post will be defined by how much in accord we are with the *Restrictive Law of Islam*. It's the 'board' that makes us upright. If we don't follow The Law, then love will become just a 'warm and fuzzy' feeling that we share with each other. We will wind up violating The Law in the name of love, and end up hurting ourselves and others.

My sincere prayer is that through this analysis we will realize that if God *is* love, and God is righteous—then the only way we can find love is by being right. If we have a 'feeling' for something or someone and it's outside of the Law of God, that is artificial love. It's not *real* love. In order for it to be real love it has to be in accord with the Law of God. Now, if the checklist of the Law of God is present, *and* that feeling is still there, then love is present. Absent the Law of God then it is just as Tina Turner once sang, a "second-hand emotion" which is not real love.

As we continue to look *at* The Law and *to* The Law, we will make the Law of God our best friend. The Law of God should be more of our friend than any Brother or Sister. Because, the minute that people find out we are not what we're talking, then what we are talking loses its credibility with that person. It is imperative that we live the character of what we talk in order for us to be *believable,* to have real *integrity* and *power*. If we are not credible when we're representing, people will say, 'he or she is fake.' This is why every time the enemy wants to make a move on a group of people; all they do is make the people *think* something negative about the person in front of them. Because as soon as they can make you think that the person in front of you is *not* what they are professing to be, then you say (in your mind) number one, "I'm justified in not being it either". And number two, "Ah, I ain't even got to". The enemy destroys the whole group by *discrediting* the one who's talking.

The Restrictive Law Is Our Success

The Restrictive Law is **our** success at all times. We want it to be every individual's success, but the word "our" is plural. This is true whether each individual *chooses* to make it *their* success or not. We must make it as a group, "our" success. We don't administer The Law on one another out of hatred for one another. The Law *is* love, and proper application of The Law is what grows us into love. When we have love, we're not disciples anymore, we're apostles. When we have love we don't need someone from the outside to impose a prohibition on us—we prohibit it from within ourselves.

The mark of a leader is self-motivation; initiative. The mark of a leader is not someone with a big title, and a big degree, and a big bank account. The mark of a leader is the person that can impose the discipline on themselves —and if you can do that then you're fit to help our people who are still yet dead or asleep that need that exterior force, so we can get out of our present condition. Our unlimited rise begins with the understanding and acceptance that *family is our true power base from which all else grows and develops.*

The Offer of High Civilization

The greatest love story ever told is not Romeo and Juliet or Jay-Z and Beyoncé or Will and Jada. The greatest love story ever told is that God left Paradise to come and unite a people in the wilderness of North America.

When there is belief in The God, Master Fard Muhammad, The Christ, The Honorable Elijah Muhammad, and The Anointed Servant, the Honorable Minister Louis Farrakhan and in the Self, we can achieve anything that we want to see accomplished.

We learn by observation of sports and all other fields of talent, that the proper preparation prevents a poor performance. When the practice of marriage is studied, we learn that for the most part, the majority of Americas are performing marriage poorly. It's not just among Black people it's also among whites.

The reason why we are now being directed by the Honorable Minister Louis Farrakhan to offer Muhammad's high civilization format for courtship, engagement and marriage is because every negative statistic that could exist among human beings, we find that America is at the top of all statistical categories.

America has more obese people, more people in prison, more hospitals because they have more sick people and more insane asylums than anywhere else on the face of the earth. There are more people that die from cancer in America than anywhere else. More people with hypertension, high blood-pressure, and more people have heart-attacks here in America. More murders in one city in America than most countries in the world. In the whole country of England last year there were less than 50 homicides, but right in Indianapolis alone over 120 in 2015. In every negative statistic that could exist among humans, America is number one. These facts alone prove one of the oft repeated sayings we have in the Nation of Islam that 'wherever the white man tells you go, stay away from' and 'wherever the white man tell you to stay away from, run to it.'

We live in a world where truth is stranger than fiction. We live in a world that is absolutely ruled and governed by Satan himself. In the scriptures (Rev. 12:9) we find that Satan who is also identified as beast or dragon also called Lucifer or the Devil who deceived the whole world. There is no more deception in the world than there is in America. America is the headquarters for Satan. This is the throne of the Satan. This is the place where Satan governs and originates all his designs to mess the whole planet up, including marriage.

The great fighter Joe Louis said when asked 'how much has boxing done for you?' His response was: 'Look let me explain something to you; champions are not made in the ring they are announced there. Before you ever get in the ring you already have to be a champion.' He also said: 'Whenever you get in the ring, everything from that point on is all a matter of reflexes. But it is the hitting of the speed bag. It is the working of the heavy bag. It is the working of the mitts, it's the road work, it's the abdominal workout, and it's the rope jump. It's all of those things that you do *before* you get in the ring that really makes you a champion. And after you get in the ring, because of the road work, because of working the mitts, the speed bag, the heavy bag, catching the medicine ball you are on reflex in the boxing ring.' It should be the same with marriage. So that whenever we do get into marriage it's all reflex from that point on.

Changing Our Mindset

Brothers and sisters you have to be a millionaire long before you ever get a million dollars? Being a millionaire is a mindset. Joe Louis said '...that champions are not made in the ring they are announced there.' That means long before he ever stepped into the ring and won the belt physically he already was a champion mentally. If you have to be a millionaire long before you have a million dollars then millionaire is a mindset long before it's six zero's at the end of a number. If we are to be successful in marriage, we have to already know what it means to be a husband, to be a father, to be a mother and to be a wife, long before we ever walk down the aisle or receive some beautiful sister's hand.

According to Jesus, anyone that tries to do anything without having gone thorough proper preparation to prevent a poor performance, he referred to them as a 'Fool that builds their house on sand' but wise people always 'build their home on solid rock'. (Matt. 7:24-26)

Why because the foundation has to support a certain amount of structural weight. When we look at the heavy weight of being a wife, the heavy weight of being a husband; and if one is a husband and a wife, what comes from those two are two new titles. Husbands and wives become fathers and mothers. What then is the weight of parents? What is the weight of two that have left their mother and their father, Jesus said, and have "cleaved unto the wife as the husband and cleaved unto the husband as the wife and the two have become one flesh?" (Matt. 19:5) How much weight is that?

When we look at the process of two people becoming one, with the expressed goal of becoming one with Allah (God) they are tasked with becoming fathers and mothers—responsible for replenishing the earth also. Replenish means to replace with something better. *This means it's our job as mothers and fathers, not to make our children like us but to make our children better than us.* Replenish the earth and subdue it.

BEFORE YOU SAY I DO

Jesus and Divorce

The word FATHER and FARTHER have the same root word. The job of the FATHER is to train up the son and the daughter to stand on his shoulders. Not stay hugged up under my arm, not stay hugged up in my house deep into adulthood, but a good father wants their child to be independent, on their own. Taking all that they have taught them, not being content to just stand beside me, but to stand on my shoulders and take the name and family legacy to a whole different level.

The reality is that divorce originated with the white man. In the Book of Matthew Chapter 19 Verse 8 of the Bible, Jesus is being questioned about divorce. The line of questing comes right after he tells them: When you get married your goal is to become one flesh—two becoming one. Many rejected what Jesus taught them because they knew that was and is no small task. When two people become one, they can communicate without words. When two people become one, they do not have to see the facial expressions of the other person because they can FEEL THEM. When two people become one, not only can they feel each other, if they're in the basement and you're in the living room, but you can feel them if they're in California and you're in New York.

When two people truly become one, they develop a spiritual bridge this allows them to communicate in a deeply intimate way. An invisible bridge, which binds the male and the female together, and it is where and how information is continuously shared without the use of facial expressions or words being necessary. This form of communication is very similar to a mother's intuition. A mother can *feel* the child. This is why even though the mother drank alcohol, smoked cigarettes, and ate pork (swine) and her blood pressure was high, she had hypertension, and was overweight; somehow she knows when you are in distress. This is possible because the mother has a built in invisible bridge that's a deep spiritual connection through which she can *feel you*, even when she hasn't heard or seen you in years.

When two become one, they begin to develop husband's intuition and wife's intuition. Where they don't have to hear you, or see your facial expressions, when they are truly one, they can feel each other. After Jesus told them that's what you're supposed to do they asked Jesus in layman's terms: 'But why did Moses say it was OK to get a divorce?' Jesus' answered by saying, 'Moses *permitted* you to divorce your wives because your hearts were hard, but it was not this way from the beginning.' In the New Living Translation it reads this way: 'It was not what God originally intended.' In God's Word Translation, the same passage reads: 'It was NEVER this way in the beginning.'

Moses (Musa) Lifts Up A Serpent

If you research this you will find that the first time divorce was ever permitted was when Moses permitted it. Which means that divorce is a 4,000 year-old concept, it only recently came into existence, but how long have we actually been on the planet? The Original Man, according to the Divine Teachings of the Honorable Elijah Muhammad, has been in existence for over 78 trillion-years. When the Honorable Elijah Muhammad, in the Theology of Time, was comparing the 6,000 years of the white man's history to the original man's history, he said that 'the white man's history in comparison to the original man's history is less than a fraction of one second compared to a whole day.' If you are conducting a mathematical comparison, examining the 4,000 years in comparison to the original time frame of 78 trillion-years, then divorce has been in existence only a 'hot second'.

The question is who was Moses a Prophet to? The Jews have almost the whole world believing that Moses was a Prophet sent to free white people from a Black Pharaoh in Egypt. Master Fard Muhammad, Allah (God) in person asked the question in the Supreme Wisdom: **"Why did Musa (Moses) have a hard time civilizing the Devil 2000 B.C.?"** and the answer in part is **"Because he was a SAVAGE"** what this means is that if the work that Moses did was to resurrect white people in the hills and cave-sides of Europe then he is a prophet to the white man. "Musa (Moses) was a half original man and a prophet." We learn from the scriptures about the history of Moses from the book of John (3:14) wherein it describes his mission. In part it reads: 'and as Moses raised a serpent up in the wilderness.'

When you look at a map, you see that there is no wilderness in the desert. What the wilderness symbolically represents is the animalistic condition that white people were found in when they were living in the hills and cave-sides of Europe. In order for Musa (Moses) to raise them up he had to teach them: how to cook, how to build a home for themselves and how to live a respectable life. He found them crawling around on their all-fours and to correct this and force them to stand upright, he had to put a board on their back. Again, Moses invented the girdle and its original purpose was not to hold the anatomy intact; it was used to keep the board in position in order to force the white man to walk upright. They didn't like the fact that the work of Moses was to civilize them. They ate their food raw before Moses taught them to cook their food.

Still to this day they will eat anything and desire their food 'rare' which really means raw. Food that is cooked 'rare' actually means they want the food with blood still present in it. Again, they will eat anything, including things that are not fit for a civilized human being to consume. They change the names of things so when you go to a fine restaurant and you order calamari you are actually ordering a baby octopus. Order escargot and you are eating Snails. Caviar, which are considered a fine delicacy, are in fact fish eggs. To take their deception even further they will chocolate cover anything. You can buy chocolate covered ants, grasshoppers and crickets. In the so-called finer restaurants they serve a desert called 'Blood-Pudding' which is made by taking cows blood, putting powdered sugar on it, mixing it with flour, and serving it like a Jell-O-Pop, but it is in fact blood. This is the level that they were and are functioning from. In fact, Honorable Elijah Muhammad teaches us that Moses had to sleep in a ring of fire because if he didn't do so they would have killed Moses.

In the true history of Moses, the raising of a serpent in the wilderness represents the civilization of Caucasian people. When we read in the Bible, that Moses permitted divorce who was he talking to? He was talking to a people who had lost the knowledge of themselves. He was speaking to a people that were living a beast life. He was instructing a people that were crawling around on their all-fours who had lost everything including the use of language. The dog was their best friend. Look at Jesus' response closely and you will see that he was actually talking to Black People: "Moses permitted you to divorce your wives because your hearts were hard, but it was not this way from the beginning." Divorce was allowed because of the weakness and wickedness of white people.

According to Biblical History, during this time instead of divorcing their wives, when they no longer desired the woman as a wife, the man would kill the woman or beat her until they ran away, some records indicate that they would have the wife falsely imprisoned. Just look at the history of King Henry VIII of England, he had four of his six wives executed. When Moses introduced divorce he was introducing this as an alternative to killing, enslaving or beating the woman, just let her go and divorce her, since your hearts are hard, since you're devils, since you're savage, since you're crazy. So you say 'Well what about us, you know we're savages too'. The question is what are you after you got your X or Muhammad? After you received your original name, after we received our original religion, after we started eating our original diet, after we started learning our original tongue (language) then it's time for us to return to the way it was in the beginning. Since divorce was not even permitted in the beginning and there was no record of it, then if we want to have healthy relationships again we need to go back to the beginning.

Accepted Vs. Original

We need to examine closely the first 'accepted' original couple, and then we can identify and study the "actual" original couple. The *accepted* original couple is according to this world's scholars, Adam and Eve; however, they are not the *"actual"* original couple, they are the *'accepted'* couple. The *'accepted'* original couple is Adam and Eve but the "ACTUAL" original couple is the Supreme Being who is Self-Created and His Second-Self.

When we closely examine the principles of what the accepted original couple was operating from we can gain some valuable guidance that can be applied to our courtship process. At the end of the day, if prior to Moses' interaction with white people there was no divorce then this indicates that the accepted original couple brought the right ingredients to the table to create a recipe for a lasting and healthy relationship. If divorce was originally permitted and now has evolved to be the acceptable norm, then clearly we are missing some essential ingredients in the process.

The Essential Ingredients

Ingredient One

One point that is often overlooked in the analysis of the accepted original couple is that they had a garden, which means, they were feeding themselves. The scientists of evil, today are selling foods that is not real food, but is in fact an industrialized commodity posing as food –fake food. Fake food chemically designed and enhanced, it's not food but in fact it is 'good tasting plastic.'

There's fluoride in the water which allows the scientists of evil to control and manipulate the thinking of the people who drink it. These evil scientists have genetically modified the seeds that grow almost all of the vegetables now. Which means, Mon-Satan or Monsanto, has put inside of the seeds a built in insecticide and the only place you can buy these insecticide infused seeds is in America because the philosophy in this country, is that anything can be sold as food as long as it has not been **proven** to be dangerous. Yes, they will knowingly feed poison to the people. The Honorable Elijah Muhammad teaches us in 'How to Eat to Live Book I, that the white man will feed you anything, "as long as it does not kill…(you)…instantly." Other countries philosophy is that 'we've got to prove that it's not dangerous **before** it's sold to the people. If it's killing the insects then what is it doing to us, to human beings? So the number one thing is they were growing their own food.

Ingredient Two

When Adam, was first created, God said: 'It is not good for man to be alone.' The reality is that a female can handle being single better than a man can. We don't have the space in this book to go any deeper into this point but I believe you already understand what I'm talking about.

Can I drop something on you sisters that are reading this? One of the things that I strongly cautioned against in an earlier chapter was that as women you *absolutely* must avoid jumping into a relationship out of neediness because once you become needy you settle—for less. Once you think you're old, you settle. Do you understand me? But the highest form of loneliness is not being by yourself, the highest form of loneliness is when you are with the wrong man. So it's better to be single sisters, than to be lonely because out of neediness you settled for the wrong man.

What's interesting though is that after God says: 'It's not good for man to be alone.' Notice the language, God doesn't say it's not good for the male to be alone; it's not good for the boy to be alone. When you look at the accepted original couple, *God made Adam a man before he ever gave him a woman.* This means that a boy doesn't need a woman. The accepted original couple was a man and a woman, not a boy and a girl. *Before two people can be married, number one a man's got to be a man, and number two the woman's got to be a woman, otherwise 'we at the crib' where babies play.* At the crib where we are boys and girls but not men and women, well that's not what marriage is for. Marriage is for a MATURE male and a MATURE female.

If God didn't send you to him until he became a man, why are you willing to be with a boy? This means sisters that your criteria should be, 'I've got to see how much of a man he is, before I'm willing to submit myself as a woman, because I'm a woman and I don't wanna be with a boy.' A man will take care of you sisters; a boy will need you to take care of him. A man knows how to handle his business, but a boy needs you to handle his business. A man can get it in his name, but a boy needs to put it in your name.

So before you give yourself over to a male sister you must make sure he's not a boy but is in fact a man, otherwise he's not qualified. Some of you sisters want to throw up the excuse of; 'we're only 'courting'! But courtship is not dating. Courtship is where we involve ourselves in the process of discovery, with the specific goal of marriage.

If you are not trying to make him your husband sisters and brothers or make her your wife then you are not supposed to be courting. We do not date in the world of God. We court. We get engaged. We get married and we live happily ever after. Inshallah, Inshallah, Inshallah!

Before Adam ever had a woman he was already a man that possessed power and dominion over the 'fish of the sea, the fowl of the air and every creeping thing that crawls on the earth'. Some of you may be thinking: 'I ain't never gonna find no man now!' Focus on the lesson which is that at the very minimum, the man is supposed to be operating in the world with a certain amount of Godhood manifested in his ability to control, govern and create something. Otherwise he's not ready sisters.

Adam had power and dominion, over the fish of the sea, fowl of the air and every creeping thing that crawls on earth. Then God said 'now I've given you all that, and you've got all that in you, now be fruitful, multiply, replenish the earth and subdue it, but before you could ever carry out those instructions you have to be made up of something.' So with power and dominion over the fish of the sea, fowl of the air and every creeping thing that crawls is a certain amount of mental and physical power which is displayed by a man **before** he's ever in a relationship. Otherwise sisters you don't want to be fruitful and you don't want to be multiplying with a man that doesn't have any power.

The Originator

Now the actual original couple is not Adam and Eve. The Most Honorable Elijah Muhammad said that 'Allah (God) was Self-Created. The mathematics that the Most Honorable Elijah Muhammad gave to us in a quick synopsis, three things were present in the universe at the point of creation: The thought of God, the material darkness, what the Holy Qur'an calls triple darkness or black mud, sounding clay, the Bible calls it dust, but dust needs water in order for it to be formed so when you put dust with water it becomes black mud or sounding clay. Again, there were only three things present; the thought of God, the material darkness and electricity. The thought of God knew how to guide the electricity to strike the material darkness at the right place, at the right time to resurrect the first atom of life. The electricity that was guided into the atom from that point on was called an electron and it is from that electron that the atom gets its positive and negative energy and power. When that atom begins revolving in space it begins to share some of its charge with the other dead atoms which had no aim or purpose. Then these atoms which had no aim and purpose connected to the 'living atom', borrowed life from that 'living atom' and atoms grew up and they became molecules. These molecules became cells and the cells kept on operating and they became an organ and that organ was the brain and from the organ called brain other organs came into existence and then an organism called body was the finished product of this self-creation.

The Most Honorable Elijah Muhammad teaches us that after Allah created Himself, He studied Himself and found in

Himself a Second-Self. You say 'well where did the earth come from?' The Honorable Elijah Muhammad said that 'Allah created His home planet simultaneous to His own self-creation. That's why when we die they say 'ashes to ashes and dust to dust', because what the earth is, we are. And what we are the earth is since we were made at the exact same time from the same material. The earth is 75% water and so is the human body. The earth has seas and oceans which are salt water and we have tears and sweat. The earth has lakes and rivers and we have blood and saliva, fresh water. The vegetation of the earth matches the molecular structure of the flesh of man, rock or earth is bone and the lakes and streams of the earth move like the veins and arteries on the planet. So when the mathematics was given to us as Actual Facts we were taught that there was one hundred thirty nine million six hundred and eighty five thousand square miles of water on the earth. But when you add up the Pacific, Atlantic, and Indian oceans, then add the lakes and rivers it adds up to one hundred and forty million, three hundred and eighty five thousand. Why? How is this possible, it's possible because there's seven hundred thousand square miles of lakes, rivers, seas and oceans that are inside the human body, we are from the earth and the earth is from us.

This is why when men give gifts to women, we give her flowers. We give them gold, we give them diamonds. Why because Allah created Himself and He created His home planet simultaneously. And after He created Himself, He found in Himself a Second-Self and brought out of Himself a Woman. And when that Woman came into existence He didn't give her a flower He gave her ALL OF THE FLOWERS. He didn't give her a diamond, He gave her ALL OF THE DIAMONDS. He didn't give her a little gold bracelet, He gave her ALL OF THE GOLD in the earth. So brothers we've been trying to duplicate what the Original God did for His wife. 'Here you go, here's a dozen roses, I ain't got my weight up yet but coming soon I'll soon get you two dozen, and pretty soon I'll get you a whole botanical garden, but right now this the best I can do. I can't do it like the Originator did so here you go, here's a ring to put on. But coming soon, I will get you all of it.' That's where the idea to give her gifts originated, it originated with The Originator.

According to the Most Honorable Elijah Muhammad, when you study the Originator and the Second-Self, you are looking at not the accepted original. You say: 'Well what was Jesus talking about?' Jesus wasn't talking about Adam and Eve. The Honorable Elijah Muhammad said that Jesus had read Al-Qur'an? Well, you know it couldn't have been the one that came with Prophet Muhammad (PBUH) because the current Holy Qur'an that came with Prophet Muhammad came six hundred years after Jesus. So how was Jesus six hundred years before Prophet Muhammad reading the Holy Qur'an? The Holy Qur'an that Jesus was reading wasn't the one hundred and fourteen chapters that were revealed to Prophet Muhammad. It was called Al-Qur'an the 'Mother Book', 'The Nations Book'; it is from that writing that present Bible and Holy Qur'an come from. That's why they are both called scriptures, as scripture means a part of a greater writing.

The Original Holy Qur'an is not one hundred and fourteen chapters. The Original Bible is not some sixty six little books. Do they house all the wisdom of God? The Bible is a six-thousand year history and the Holy Qur'an is just a little bit more than that. But the Originators, the Scientist, used to make or write history twenty-five thousand years in advance, so when Jesus was reading Al-Qur'an, he was not studying the acceptable definition of the beginning—Adam and Eve. His definition of 'the beginning' wasn't based on Adam and Eve, it was based on 'the beginning' of the first God and His Second-Self.

The Characteristics of a Real Man

Yes, we get a few jewels from Adam; we get some good principles from Eve, because she came into existence to be a helpmeet, not a help-mate. See help-mate means that she's a sexual object (help-*mate*) but help*meet* means that she's supposed to be connected to a man in order to help him fulfill his goals, dreams and aspirations, purpose and mission for living. A man that does not know where he's going does not need any help getting there. A Helpmeet not help-mate.

The Originator, let's look closely the characteristics of the Original First Husband. The Honorable Elijah Muhammad says that the Self-Created God, He waged war on the darkness. So the first characteristic of a real man is that he must be a warrior. Any man that will not operate in the world with the mindset of a warrior and a soldier, when you're Black in America if you're not a soldier then you are gonna be a punk and a cheap man for life. Because we live in a world diametrically opposed to the Black man's rise. So don't get up and talk like white people Black man. 'I'm going to make me a to-do list today. I'm going to write out my goals and objectives for Tuesday.' No white people can do that because this is their world. When you wake up in the morning don't make a 'to-do list' make a battle plan. That's what warriors do. And it's something about language, when you think 'to-do list' or 'goal-sheet' but when you say 'battle plan' you think, life and death. So in the subconscious, the mind says: 'Look if you don't make a certain amount of money, you're going to die. If you don't get that task done, you might die. If you don't achieve that objective then your enemies will have the upper hand on you tomorrow.'

When you think like a warrior and make a battle plan, then you move through the world, quick thinking, fast moving, clean inside and out, right down to the modern times, trying to win a war. So the first characteristic of a real man is he's got to be a warrior. The real truth is that don't no woman want a punk a man, she might get mad at you, mad at you for cussing em out, mad at you for smackin' the taste outta somebody's mouth, but in the quiet of the room she's back there laughing, because at the end of the day she wants to know when it goes down, that 'I gotta man that will push me to the back and handle business kill and die for me.' That's a warrior.

If Allah created His home planet simultaneously, that means that the Original Man had to have a vision. He had to already have a blueprint in His mind of what the earth needed to look like and be made of in order to sustain Himself, His Second-Self and from these two there would spread many men and women into the Billions and maybe Trillions one day of people. So a real man has to be a man that has a vision.

What is a vision? A vision is your image of the future. Vision is the minds ability to leave your body in present time, take a tour of your future, record notes of what it sees, then come back to your body and use what it has seen to inspire you in present time to go to work to bring what you saw into existence in the now. A man without a vision is not a man.

Next, this man was a Producer. Look at all the trees He made. Look at what He produced. Everything we see He produced. So when you are looking for good man sisters or brothers if you want to be a man, then you've got to be a producer.

He also had to be hard working and organized. Do you know how long the Original man worked? The Most Honorable Elijah Muhammad says it took Him Trillions of years. The Honorable Minister Louis Farrakhan said it like this: "It took Him eons, and eons of time." That's a long time. Not only was He hard working and organized, He had to have patience and perseverance. He didn't quit when He got tired, He quit when He was done. That's a real man. A real man has to be hard working. A real man has to be patient. A real man has to have perseverance and a real man has to be organized. You cannot be dirty and be organized at the same time. There is no such thing a filthy organization.

Brothers, whenever we start thinking about this thing called: 'I do!' We should be making sure we have already married these principles before we try to marry a person. Have you married the principle of being a warrior? A man of vision? A producer? A hard working, patient, persevering, clean, organized man? Until you've married these principles you don't need somebody else. And when sisters start thinking about what the characteristics are that you should be looking for to determine whether or not you should even think about him…there it is.

NURI MUHAMMAD

The Second-Self

Look at what His Second-Self was. Now what was so beautiful, according to the history, the Second-Self was **with** The Originator. The Honorable Elijah Muhammad was asked one time: 'Well, did the Black woman, did she come into existence after the moon?' and The Honorable Elijah Muhammad said: "There never was a time when the Black man was without his woman." The person then asked: '…What about like maybe the stars, because sixty-six trillion years ago moon but stars was coming into existence around seventy-two trillion years ago.' He said: "Brother there never was a time that the Black man was without his woman." Well how do you calculate time? It's by the sun. So if there never was a time and time is calculated by the sun, before the sun was, the Black woman was here. That means Black woman that the Second-Self of Allah was working with her husband in a cold dark environment and did not complain. We have no record of complaint. When you marry a man or a woman you're marrying onto part *present person* and you're marrying another part, *potential person*. Our problem is that we are marrying too much potential and not enough present. You at least want to have most of the present there and then some thirty percent potential that can be worked on as time goes on. But in your mind when you think: 'I'm gonna be the one, I'm gonna make this man into something, he's just never been loved. After I put this good…this good meal on him, a couple of these rub downs…' No, you better let God make a man out of him before you make a husband out of him. Otherwise prepare for hell.

Here you are marrying a man or a woman off of seventy percent potential person and only thirty percent present, what are they supposed to be and you just got married and both of you forty-five. This means for the last forty-five years they've never developed those potentials and you think that after you married them that in the next six months, all of a sudden Iron Man Muhammad will be here. Wonder Woman 3X will be here? If they haven't been able to develop it in forty-five years, what makes you think they will develop it in the few months or a few years after they get married?

When you are marrying one part potential person and hopefully a larger part present person then you must be willing to work with him as he's trying to get something off the ground. That's what a cold dark environment represents. Help him to get it going sisters.

Look at what else The Honorable Minister Louis Farrakhan said about this Second-Self, he said: "When Allah created her, He created her to fulfill certain desires…" look at this. Min. Farrakhan said: "He (The Creator) did not need a woman, He wanted one…" 'He did not need her, He wanted her.' That's why the male is more magnetized by the female, than female is to the male. You don't believe me? Then let me give you a real world example. They have a place that sells chicken wings, it's called 'Hooters', you've never seen a chicken wing spot called 'Biceps", now have you? Go buy a woman's magazine and then go buy a men's magazine. When you open up a woman's magazine they got makeup tricks, recipes, articles about how to de-stress. But you open up a man's magazine, on page two there's a naked woman, page six another naked woman, there's just naked women all in there but why? It's because whenever Allah created Himself, He brought out of Himself His Second-Self so the female is a perfect figure of the imagination of The Originator. So whenever the man created his woman, he made her to look, smell and feel exactly like he wanted. So when he sees her, it moves him more than when she sees him, because at the end of the day he brought her in, she didn't bring him in. Think on that.

Min. Farrakhan said that He (The Originator) also wanted: "wanted something that He could look at that would be kind to his eye." First form of consolation sisters is the way you keep yourself and the greatest way to keep yourself is found in the words of The Honorable Elijah Muhammad: "That your beauty sisters really is in your weight." If you keep yourself at your ideal weight and you multiplied that by a smile and a good personality, I don't care what you look like; you will be a beautiful woman, guaranteed.

Then he said that: 'He wanted her to comfort Him and console Him while He was at war with the darkness." Man! Consolation! Now I was typing the word 'consolation' and I guess I haven't typed it enough, so anything you type a lot is automatically spell checked. So consolation was corrected to a word that really describes what a lot of times relationships end up doing. It replaced it with 'cancellation'. You are supposed to offer consolation not cancellation. Cancellation is 'You ain't nothin', 'You are worthless, you are lazy. I shoulda known, ya mama told me, where you going, you still lying.' You see that's cancellation. Consolation number one comes from your appearance sisters, keeping self-up. Next it is complimenting your man. Did you know that men operate and their language reflects a base where honor (respect) is of the most critical importance? Honor, but the female's language is security? A woman cannot be a good woman if she's in an insecure situation. If she's not for sure whether the lights are going to be on, or the waters going to be on, or are we getting ready to get kicked out, she's not going to be able to be the woman she's supposed to be.

Likewise, if a man doesn't have a woman that believes in him, that's willing to feed him some honor, which is how women take men and how men take other people's women. 'Sugar-Daddy' shows up. Right? 'I've been seeing you struggling; now I don't want anything. No just take this...' Next thing you know she comes to you brothers: 'You are such a fine man, have you been working out?' 'Yes ma'am I've been curling Subway sandwiches.' And then your mind starts saying: 'My wife don't never notice nothin! This is a brand-new suit, she didn't even know I got a new suit. But LaQuesha at the job, she noticed my cufflinks.' You see that's honor.

Now, the other form of consolation is being clean. A woman loses beauty when she is not a clean person. Another aspect of consolation is being kind. Understand where I'm going with this? *Keep yourself up, compliment him, and be clean.* A lot of C's and K's in here. Kind and can cook. If you got: Can Cook, is Kind, is Clean, is Complementary and Keeps herself up, then you've got the Second-Self of God. And that's what you brothers should be looking for whenever you think about a wife. Present person vs potential person.

The Honorable Minister Louis Farrakhan also teaches that: "He (The Originator) needed someone that He could talk to about His desires, and who would help Him to meet His objectives." That means that if you want be a good woman you cannot be a dumb woman. No one can talk to you about desires if you don't have intelligence. Next he says: "He (The Originator) needs a helper, not just any helper a big helper, but big in mind not in body." That's the words of The Minister Louis Farrakhan.

When the math is done brothers and sisters, we can take a few jewels and nuggets from Adam and Eve, but in the beginning it was not so. In the beginning it never was intended to be getting together then getting divorced. In the beginning, we were supposed to be together for the rest of our lives until we became one flesh and we became one with the Supreme Being. That's the way it was supposed to be. And the only way we are going to get it right is if we go back to doing it like we did it in the beginning. So as men let us strive hard to be that Self-Created God and as women let us strive hard to be that Second-Self of God. And even if you don't have and we don't have ALL of the present person, the least we can do is work on the potential person to help each other get there and as time goes on more of the real ingredients that make a relationship will come into play, and the better the relationship will get.

Epilogue

If you are a part of any religion and the goal of the religion is just to make you into a worshipper, or a believer, or a follower—or even a saint, an apostle, a companion, then you need to change your religion. Because "religion", by definition, is supposed to be a spiritual process that re-"again" (does something again) "ligion" (gets to God) gets us back into Oneness with God.

We thank Allah for a man that has set an example on how to become **One with God**. And not only did he set the example, but he gave us the explanation on how we, in fact, can follow in his footsteps. For this reason and for so many more we thank Allah (God) and the Eternal Leader of the Nation of Islam, the Most Honorable Elijah Muhammad for blessing us with The Honorable Minister Louis Farrakhan.

All Praises Are Due to Allah!

NURI MUHAMMAD

Direct Words of Guidance From The Honorable Minister Louis Farrakhan

Properly starting a courtship

When an FOI sees an MGT that he thinks will make him a good wife, he should mention this to the Minister, Brother Captain, or Lieutenant to find out if she is available. A brother should never approach an MGT to inquire about her marital status or interest in him. He should not hint or flirt. If he hasn't already been introduced, he should ask to be introduced to her (however, it not recommended that you go into courtship with a complete stranger with whom you've never as much as shared a conversation). The request (to find out her availability) is forwarded to the Sister Captain. If the sister being requested declines and does not wish to court, the Brother Captain will inform the FOI and he moves on. If she accepts, a meeting will be arranged for them to formally meet and counsel them on the rules of courtship.[1]

Can a sister ask for a brother in courtship?

Likewise, if a sister sees a brother that she is interested in finding out more about, she would go to her sister Captain and make that known. The Sister Captain would then approach the brother Captain and he would make this known to the brother. If the brother is interested in the sister, (the sister asking about knowing him better), then the two of them can meet and begin the process of learning about each other.[1]

---

[1] Courtship Interview, Phoenix, AZ June 30, 2006

Is permission and/or approval needed to Court someone?

No one's permission or approval is needed to court someone although out of courtesy, one should inform the Laborers. The Laborers are informed by going through the above mentioned process; however, this process should not be misinterpreted to mean that you must wait for permission. No official should deliberately block a Believer from courtship and no Laborer has any authority over who a Believer chooses to court. If the Laborers have concerns about someone, they should arrange to meet the brother and/or sister and share their concerns. However, an official should not try to control or unduly interfere in the personal business or courtship process of any Believer. [2]

How long should a brother be in the Mosque before asking for a sister?

If a sister has been in the Mosque for a significant amount of time and the brother is just coming in and he sees a sister, it is better not to court. Let that brother get trained in the way of God for at least 3 - 9 months. A sister cannot take a chance on marrying someone who just popped up out of the grave because you are putting yourself under the authority of someone who will not have the wisdom to guide a wife and family. Let that person come into the Nation and get grounded in the way of Allah and the Messenger, then it would be proper

---

[2] [Courtship Interview, Atlanta, GA May, 2005 & webcast June 30, 2006]

to court. But just to scope a person coming in that you saw accept the faith, then you want to start courting—that is not wise. [3]

Should the Courtship be announced to the Believers?

No, courtships are private and should not be announced. The engagement is public and it should be announced.[4]

Does Courtship include pre-marital sex?

Absolutely not. As soon as sex is introduced, the courtship is over. Because of the intoxicating influence of sex, one's judgment will be clouded, thus affecting one's ability to make a sound, sober decision.[1]

"Courtship is very serious, courtship should not be entered into with the frivolous mind of two persons coming out of the grave, who have had a lot of sexual intimacy and now they are in the Nation of Islam where fornication and adultery is forbidden. So, out of necessity or biological pressure to have sex we enter into courtship not to find out whether the person is worthy of my hand in marriage, but we enter into courtship to fulfill some biological need, which destroys the process of what courtship is all about. And most of the times the persons enter into a sexual relationship which blinds them to the true purpose of courting and then either one gets pregnant or then they decide after having sex with each other that they don't really want to

---

[3] [Courtship Interview with the Honorable Minister Louis Farrakhan, Phoenix, AZ June 30, 2006]

[4] [Courtship Interview with the Honorable Minister Louis Farrakhan, Atlanta, GA May, 2005]

be with each other and then they step apart. This is very much against the law and teachings of the Honorable Elijah Muhammad and Islam. (In some cases they may feel guilty)....yes, (with) the guilt feeling of breaking the law rather than taking the time (out) for such an offense, we feel the necessity then to get married and the marriage is doomed to failure because it has started improperly.

Courtship has no involvement with kissing, and petting. It has no involvement with anything but a serious quest to learn about the individual so that one can make an intelligent, sober decision as to getting engaged to be married."[5]

What is the Nation of Islam's view of older sister/younger brother in Courtship? How old should they be?

The age of majority, 18? It is not just (about) the age of majority because 18 years of age does not necessarily signify maturity. These are decisions that must be made by people of mature thinking, advised and counseled by wise and mature spiritual guides.[4]

How long should courtship last? 3 months? 6 months? 1 year? Or...?

I would not put a time limit on courtship. When we go to court, our aim is to find evidence that either convicts or frees the accused—long trials are expensive. Long courtships are of no value. Courtship should be only as long as it takes the parties involved to find the necessary truths about each other that

---

[5] [Courtship Interview with the Honorable Minister Louis Farrakhan, Phoenix, AZ June 30, 2006]

either say the courtship should be ended or that the two should become engaged to be married.[4]

How long should a person wait after a courtship has ended, before entering into another courtship?

Courtship is not the serious commitment—you're not making a commitment to an individual when you say I'm interested in discovery of whether or not you would be the person that I would like to become engaged to. If there is no sex, no disrespect of that person, no kissing, no petting, no nothing, then you owe nothing to one another so if at any time you decide that this is not right for you, you can cut that loose because the emotional aspect of this is not triggered through courtship. The emotional aspect is triggered when the courtship process is leading to strong, intense feelings about one another. Then, when that breaks down, the emotional impact of the breaking of a courtship that has gone to that emotional stage, then time should be required to heal from the emotional strain of a break up before we get involved in another courtship.[6]

---

[6] [Courtship Interview with the Honorable Minister Louis Farrakhan, Phoenix, AZ June 30, 2006]

What is the proper way to end a courtship?

If the person asks for details, be truthful. However, if the questioning becomes counterproductive, excessive, and obsessive, encourage him/her to seek counseling and/or talk with their Captain. Both parties should also inform their parents/families that the courtship has ended just as they did in the beginning of the courtship. Hopefully the Laws of Islam have been followed during the process of discovery, the courtship ends amicably, and the community of the brotherhood and sisterhood is preserved with no ill feelings on either side.[7]

I am encountering difficulties in my courtship, is that a sign that I should end it?

"...All of us need help, No Black person in America is without a problem. This is a problem world so when you marry, you marry a problem that has to be solved. Beautiful problem, but a problem."[8]

During the courtship process, problems that are discussed and come up should be seen as a hurdle to be overcome. If you find someone who has the basic characteristics that you are looking for and would make a good husband or wife, then use maturity, wisdom, and skill to address these problems. In every relationship, there are bound to be difficulties that come up and handling these difficulties will help prepare you for overcoming problems in marriage. Reflect on the stages of

---

[7] [Honorable Minister Louis Farrakhan]

[8] [Hon. Min. Louis Farrakhan, "How to Mend/Heal a Broken Heart, Pt. II]

relationships and be sure that you are not ending part of a difficulty factor that comes naturally in all relationships.[9]

Suppose you are courting someone and they are placed in F-time, what happens to the Courtship?

The courtship ends. If someone is placed in F time and that signifies either fornication, adultery, gross hypocrisy or rebellion, why would a sister in good standing want to marry a brother who goes into F time? Well 90 days for smoking or 90 days for drinking or 90 days for smoking reefer or 90 days for gambling, then when you see a person you are courting and they are found guilty of infractions of the law; then you are learning something more about the person, that should influence your decision making process. The courtship stops if the person does the time, if it is 90 days, but if it 1-5, that courtship is over. But if it is a 90 day or 30 day or 60 day then the courtship stops but when that person has fulfilled their obligation with respect to time and comes back to the Mosque and is once again in good standing then if the person decides then the courtship can continue.[7]

The role of Chaperones

"Among the righteous courtship is chaperoned. This is done to keep the parties who are attracted to each other from entering into premarital sex, which then stops the process of courtship."
- Min. Louis Farrakhan

---

[9] Courtship Interview with the Honorable Minister Louis Farrakhan, Phoenix, AZ June 30, 2006]

Courting/dating outside the NOI

If you see, and that goes for the sister as well, if you see a sister, you invite her to the Mosque and you watch to see if she truly desires to become a registered follower of the Honorable Elijah Muhammad. Never make a promise to her that if she becomes a Muslim you'll think about marrying her. No! You see whether Islam is attractive to her, because if you are sincere as a Muslim, you want the woman that you marry to be as sincere in her confession of faith and there should be no thought, no hint that you are bringing her to the Mosque considering that if she becomes a Muslim you will marry her because this is an inducement that is improper.[10]

Is it proper to assist the person you are courting with paying their bills?

No, No, No, it is not proper to pay bills. If the person you are courting needs assistance, this should be brought to their Captain discreetly so assistance can be given through the Mosque. Courtship is not an obligation or commitment where one must pay bills for one's court-mate. In addition, this could set up unhealthy future precedence and expectations which could cloud the judgment of both.[8]

---

[10] [Courtship Interview with the Honorable Minister Louis Farrakhan, Phoenix, AZ June 30, 2006]

Is it proper to give and/or accept gifts during courtship from the person you are courting?

Giving personal or expensive gifts is discouraged for the same reasons given above, particularly in regards to precedence and expectations. You don't give gifts to the judge. If you give a gift to the judge and the judge accepts it that is bribing the judge for a decision. Courtship is not about gift giving. Courtship is about the serious business of discovery of one another. The giving of gifts is a no-no in courtship.[11]

At what point should your children be introduced to the person you are courting?

Courtship is not a serious commitment that involves the family. Courtship is finding out about that person. If in finding out about each other, you are now thinking about getting engaged but not yet ready, you introduce that person that you are courting, that you are seriously thinking about being engaged to, to your family because this is another way of seeing what kind of father this brother is going to be, what kind of mother this sister is going to be to the children they will ultimately have responsibility over. So, it's wiser not in the initial stages of courting, but when the parties are getting serious about each other and intend to be engaged, it is then that you offer another aspect of discovery by bringing that person into a relationship with your children to see how they will mesh with your children, how the children mesh with them because all of this should impact the decision for engagement and marriage.[9]

---

[11] [Courtship Interview with the Honorable Minister Louis Farrakhan, Phoenix, AZ June 30, 2006]

At what point do I ask about whether the person has been tested for STDs (sexually transmitted diseases) or has an STD?

You can start right off. You are asking questions. It's about discovery. One should not be timid in raising those kinds of questions for discovery. But if you are so hard up and you feel that you shouldn't ask a question because you will drive the person away from you then you are not serious about what courtship should involve. At any time that you sit down with a person that you are talking to and considering engagement and ultimately marriage, you can ask the question about sexually transmitted diseases, you can ask questions about their education, you can ask questions about their health, you can ask questions about their growing up, you can ask questions about their home life, their family life, you want to know as much about that person as you can before making any serious commitment.[12]

---

[12] [Courtship Interview with the Honorable Minister Louis Farrakhan, Phoenix, AZ June 30, 2006]

INDEX

Ability 11, 16, 17, 38, 50, 77, 84, 97
Achieve 11, 22, 62, 83
Act 22, 33, 42, 48
Actions 1, 10, 12, 19, 21
Adam 73, 76, 77, 78, 79, 81, 82, 83, 91
Adultery 40, 97, 101
Advice 36, 37, 39
Allah 1, 2, 3, 5, 6, 7, 9, 10, 28, 37, 38, 48, 54, 59, 66, 69, 79, 80, 84, 87, 88, 89, 93, 96
Alone 5, 26, 28, 30, 63, 76
America 3, 17, 32, 51, 53, 54, 62, 63, 75, 83, 100
Apostle 55, 93
Apostles 55, 61
Approval 36, 96
Authority 36, 48, 96
Avoid 29, 56, 57, 76
Bad 19, 20, 22, 27, 44
Beast 49, 50, 51, 63, 71
Beautiful 44, 65, 87, 89, 100
Bed-mate 35
Beginning 17, 21, 68, 71, 72, 82, 91, 100
Belief 37, 62
Believe 11, 46, 76, 88
Bible 7, 12, 18, 21, 51, 67, 71, 79, 81

Biological 10, 28, 97
Black 1, 5, 6, 11, 12, 17, 32, 42, 43, 50, 51, 53, 62, 69, 71, 79, 83, 87, 100
Body 11, 55, 56, 79, 80, 84, 91
Born 1, 3, 6, 9, 49
Boyfriend 12, 40
Brain 48, 56, 79
Brother 17, 27, 35, 36, 37, 39, 41, 42, 60, 87, 95, 96, 98, 101, 103
Brothers 5, 10, 16, 17, 30, 31, 37, 42, 65, 77, 81, 84, 85, 90, 91
Build 11, 26, 50, 53, 65, 70
Captain 35, 95, 100, 102
Caucasian 50, 53, 54, 71
Change 55, 56, 70, 93
Chaperone 41, 42
Chaperoned 15, 16, 17, 101
Children 5, 11, 18, 22, 26, 30, 31, 43, 44, 49, 50, 51, 66, 103
Christianity 53
Church 6, 19, 53
Civilization 42, 62, 71
Clean 11, 84, 85, 90
Club-hopper 45
Commitment 99, 102, 103, 104

Compatibility 33, 35
Complain 21, 87
Conversation 7, 9, 29, 36, 95
Cook 11, 49, 50, 70, 90
Couple 1, 73, 75, 76, 79, 87
Court 16, 29, 33, 36, 37, 40, 44, 77, 95, 96, 97, 98
Courting 2, 22, 33, 39, 42, 43, 44, 77, 97, 101, 102, 103
Courtship 32, 33, 34, 35, 36, 38, 39, 40, 41, 42, 43, 44, 45, 62, 73, 77, 95, 96, 97, 98, 99, 100, 101, 102, 103, 104
Creator 6, 10, 88
Critical 1, 5, 12, 34, 90
Cultivate 10, 22, 33
Daddy 19, 20
Dating 2, 33, 34, 77, 102
Daughter 17, 19, 43, 67
Daughters 12, 18, 43
Decision 5, 30, 33, 38, 41, 42, 43, 49, 97, 98, 101, 103
Demand 15
Desire 5, 9, 38, 49, 70
Desperation 28
Development 28, 54, 55
Discipline 30, 46, 55, 56, 61
Disciplined 45, 46, 55
Discovery 33, 41, 43, 77, 99, 100, 103, 104
Disease 41, 53

Divine 2, 5, 39, 59, 69
Divorce 16, 17, 21, 25, 29, 32, 67, 68, 69, 71, 72, 73
Economic 30
Elijah 3, 6, 18, 32, 35, 50, 51, 53, 54, 59, 62, 69, 70, 75, 79, 80, 81, 83, 85, 87, 89, 93, 98, 102
Emotional 25, 39, 40, 99
Encourage 2, 37, 100
Engage 33, 38
Engaged 33, 43, 77, 98, 99, 103
Engagement 38, 43, 44, 62, 97, 103, 104
Environment 19, 53, 87, 88
Evaluate 25, 26
Excuse 19, 30, 48, 77
Expensive 42, 44, 98, 103
Ex's 23
Facebook 23
Failure 19, 59, 98
Faith 37, 97, 102
Family 1, 5, 6, 11, 12, 19, 20, 31, 38, 54, 61, 67, 96, 103, 104
Fard 3, 59, 62, 69
Farrakhan 1, 4, 21, 25, 26, 28, 33, 34, 35, 36, 37, 38, 39, 40, 41, 42, 43, 44, 54, 56, 62, 85, 88, 89, 90, 91, 93, 95, 97, 98, 99, 100, 101, 102, 103, 104

Father 5, 11, 17, 31, 65, 67, 103
Fathers 11, 31, 65, 66
Feel 28, 30, 45, 46, 67, 68, 89, 98, 104
Feeling 16, 39, 59, 60, 98
Female 5, 11, 12, 13, 22, 26, 45, 67, 76, 88, 89
Feminine 10
Financial 10, 25
Fornication 40, 42, 97, 101
Free 18, 44, 47, 51, 69
Friend 3, 27, 60, 71
Fulfill 10, 83, 88, 97
Future 1, 2, 84, 102
Garden 75, 81
Generation 19, 20
Generational 18, 19, 20
Genetics 19
Girlfriend 12, 40
God 1, 2, 3, 4, 5, 6, 9, 10, 12, 18, 19, 22, 26, 28, 31, 32, 37, 38, 45, 47, 48, 49, 51, 54, 60, 62, 66, 68, 69, 76, 77, 78, 79, 81, 82, 83, 87, 90, 91, 93, 96
Granddaddy 31
Grandma 17, 19, 31
Grandmamma 19, 20, 31
Grow 10, 54, 55, 56, 75
Grown 39, 44
Growth 53, 54, 56
Guard 11, 42
Guilty 40, 98, 101
Habits 19, 20
Heal 20, 40, 99, 100
Health 11, 20, 104
Heart 17, 29, 49, 100
Hell 3, 13, 16, 25, 27, 29, 87
Help 10, 22, 39, 40, 43, 61, 83, 88, 91, 100
Her 10, 11, 13, 16, 19, 20, 22, 23, 27, 35, 37, 59, 68, 71, 77, 80, 81, 87, 88, 89, 95, 100, 102
Him 3, 7, 10, 16, 19, 20, 23, 27, 35, 37, 43, 46, 76, 77, 83, 85, 87, 88, 89, 90, 91, 95, 100
Home 11, 31, 50, 53, 65, 70, 80, 84, 104
Honorable 1, 3, 4, 6, 18, 21, 25, 26, 27, 28, 32, 33, 34, 35, 36, 37, 38, 39, 40, 41, 42, 43, 44, 50, 51, 53, 54, 56, 59, 62, 69, 70, 75, 79, 80, 81, 83, 85, 87, 88, 89, 90, 93, 95, 97, 98, 99, 100, 101, 102, 103, 104
House 13, 22, 31, 34, 37, 46, 55, 65, 67, 81
Human 1, 4, 5, 11, 31, 47, 48, 49, 51, 54, 62, 70, 75, 80
Husband 33, 37, 40, 65, 77, 83, 87, 100

Hypertension 19, 20, 62, 68
Hypocrites 31
Ignorance 18, 19
Immature 26
Important 5, 6, 10, 11, 44, 50
Income 30
Instinct 47
Instinctively 47
Interdependent 13
Interest 9, 17, 27, 35, 39, 95
Interested 27, 35, 49, 95, 99
Intimacy 97
Intimate 25, 67
Intoxicated 38
Islam 32, 54, 59, 63, 93, 97, 98, 100, 102
Jealous 27
Jesus 4, 12, 21, 49, 55, 65, 67, 68, 71, 81, 82
Journey 12, 15
Judgement 33, 38
Justify 19, 28
Kissing 38, 42, 98, 99
Knowledge 15, 17, 18, 50, 54, 71
Laborer 36, 96
Laborers 36, 38, 41, 96
Law 19, 45, 46, 47, 48, 49, 54, 55, 56, 59, 60, 61, 98, 101
Laws 2, 16, 30, 54, 57, 59, 100
Leadership 59

Learn 1, 2, 15, 17, 41, 49, 59, 62, 69, 98
Legal 15, 33
License 13, 15, 16, 32
Life 6, 10, 11, 12, 16, 17, 19, 22, 28, 44, 45, 50, 54, 57, 70, 71, 79, 83, 104
Love 10, 17, 18, 26, 33, 39, 45, 46, 47, 54, 55, 56, 59, 60, 61, 62
Loves 9, 46
Loving 7
Loyal 46
Lying 53, 89
Male 5, 11, 13, 22, 45, 67, 76, 77, 88
Mama 19, 20, 43, 44, 89
Marriage 5, 13, 16, 17, 18, 21, 22, 25, 26, 32, 33, 38, 43, 44, 45, 62, 63, 64, 65, 76, 77, 97, 98, 100, 103, 104
Marriages 5, 18
Married 13, 15, 17, 21, 22, 25, 26, 29, 39, 44, 45, 67, 76, 77, 85, 88, 98, 99
Marry 17, 22, 33, 35, 37, 43, 85, 87, 100, 101, 102
Masculine 10
Mate 5, 10, 22, 29, 35, 40, 45
Maturity 26, 35, 39, 98, 100
Men 2, 10, 12, 50, 51, 55, 76, 80, 84, 90, 91

Momma 6, 17, 19
Money 7, 9, 11, 15, 26, 30, 83
Mother 5, 6, 9, 12, 26, 30, 31, 43, 47, 56, 65, 67, 68, 81, 103
Mothers 12, 31, 65, 66
Motive 21, 22, 27, 37
Muhammad 1, 2, 3, 4, 6, 8, 10, 12, 14, 16, 18, 20, 22, 24, 26, 28, 30, 32, 34, 35, 36, 38, 40, 42, 44, 46, 48, 50, 51, 52, 53, 54, 56, 58, 59, 60, 62, 64, 66, 68, 69, 70, 71, 72, 74, 75, 76, 78, 79, 80, 81, 82, 83, 84, 85, 86, 87, 88, 89, 90, 92, 93, 94, 96, 98, 100, 102, 104
Nation 32, 34, 39, 63, 93, 96, 97, 98
Natural 21, 27, 30, 47
Nature 10, 39, 47, 48, 55, 56
Neediness 10, 30, 76
Needy 10, 30, 76
Negative 5, 60, 62, 63, 79
Obligations 25
Original 4, 12, 53, 59, 69, 70, 71, 72, 73, 75, 76, 79, 81, 83, 84, 85
Partner 22, 27
Pay 26, 42, 102
Paying 16, 25, 42, 102
Perfect 1, 2, 10, 17, 89

Permit 15, 17
Personal 9, 10, 37, 42, 59, 96, 103
Physical 11, 25, 47, 53, 78
Physically 50, 53, 65
Pleasure 10, 56, 57
Potential 17, 87, 88, 90, 91
Power 3, 6, 12, 13, 20, 60, 61, 77, 78, 79
Prayer 4, 60
Pre-marital 38, 42, 97
Pressure 19, 20, 68, 97
Principles 57, 73, 83, 85
Problems 5, 22, 23, 100
Process 25, 27, 32, 33, 37, 42, 43, 66, 73, 77, 93, 95, 96, 97, 99, 100, 101
Proper 5, 11, 27, 35, 42, 46, 61, 62, 65, 96, 100, 102, 103
Puppy 39
Purpose 10, 17, 22, 34, 70, 79, 83, 97
Questions 15, 18, 34, 35, 41, 104
Qur'an 2, 6, 7, 12, 53, 79, 81
Rational 38, 49
Reason 19, 22, 25, 26, 27, 28, 29, 30, 44, 48, 62, 93
Reasons 10, 22, 25, 103

Relationship 1, 2, 5, 6, 9, 10, 18, 22, 23, 25, 27, 28, 29, 30, 31, 32, 34, 43, 73, 76, 78, 91, 97, 100, 103
Relationships 2, 5, 11, 15, 23, 31, 42, 72, 89, 101
Religion 5, 71, 93
Reptilian 1, 49, 54
Respectful 50, 53
Responsibility 16, 25, 103
Restrictive 30, 54, 59, 61
Revelation 49
Righteous 2, 55, 60, 101
Righteousness 46
Rules 16, 32, 44, 56, 57, 59, 95
Salvation 3, 5, 10
Savage 50, 54, 69, 71
Scripture 12, 18, 49, 51, 53, 81
Self 13, 50, 62
Self-analysis 29
Self-esteem 28
Self-mastery 30
Separated 25, 29
Separation 25, 26
Sex 1, 22, 23, 38, 42, 49, 97, 99, 101
Sexed 39
Sister 35, 36, 37, 39, 41, 60, 77, 95, 96, 98, 101, 102, 103
Son 43, 51, 53, 67

Sons 12, 18, 43
Spiritual 9, 10, 11, 22, 39, 54, 55, 67, 68, 93, 98
Spouse 29, 33
Spouses 5
Study 11, 15, 16, 17, 18, 28, 45, 48, 56, 73, 81
Success 3, 54, 59, 61
Supreme 5, 6, 9, 49, 59, 69, 73, 91
Sustain 10, 19, 84
Thirsty 28, 30
Together 25, 36, 44, 67, 91
Touching 38, 40
True 1, 10, 21, 28, 35, 61, 71, 97
Trust 16, 22
Truth 5, 11, 13, 16, 27, 29, 33, 41, 47, 63, 84
Unattractive 46
Uncle 6, 31
Uncles 5, 31
Understanding 34, 47, 49, 61
Unemployed 30
Unhappily 22, 25
Unhappy 45
Value 16, 28, 56, 98
Violating 57, 59
Wait 6, 40, 47, 96, 99
Warm 16, 59
Wedding 16, 17, 18, 44, 45

Wife 6, 10, 12, 17, 33, 35, 40, 65, 71, 77, 81, 90, 95, 96, 100
Wisdom 49, 59, 69, 81, 96, 100
Wise 39, 65, 97, 98
Woman 1, 3, 10, 11, 12, 13, 17, 23, 35, 37, 38, 43, 48, 49, 53, 71, 76, 77, 80, 84, 87, 88, 89, 90, 91, 102
Womb 9
Women 10, 30, 76, 80, 84, 89, 90, 91
Wooing 33
Worst 22, 23, 45
Wrong 9, 22, 47, 48, 50, 56, 76
Young 5, 27, 35, 39, 43, 50
Younger 35, 39, 98

About The Author

Born on November 21, 1974, Brother Nuri Muhammad joined the Nation of Islam in 1992 at seventeen years of age. Having a strong will and mind and a desire to do something positive for himself, his family and his people, Brother Nuri was consistently active in all aspects of the Mosque and became a fervent student of the Teachings of the Most Honorable Elijah Muhammad.

In August of 2005, the Honorable Minister Louis Farrakhan referred to Brother Nuri as anointed and gave him the Holy Name "Nuri," which comes from Al-Nur, meaning "the light."

Brother Nuri cherishes July 5 as the anniversary of his marriage to his wife Sis. Terri Muhammad, who is his greatest support in The Mission. They are the proud parents of three children.

For more on Nuri Muhammad visit his website: **http://www.NuriMuhammad.com/ or twitter @Nuri1974**

Concordance of Scriptures

Jeremiah 1:5 – Pg 9

NLT – ⁵ "I knew you before I formed you in your mother's womb. Before you were born I set you apart and appointed you as my prophet to the nations."

GW – ⁵ "Before I formed you in the womb, I knew you. Before you were born, I set you apart for my holy purpose. I appointed you to be a prophet to the nations."

KJV – ⁵ Before I formed thee in the belly I knew thee; and before thou camest forth out of the womb I sanctified thee, and I ordained thee a prophet unto the nations.

Hosea 4:6 – Pg 18

NLT – ⁶ My people are being destroyed because they don't know me. Since you priests refuse to know me, I refuse to recognize you as my priests. Since you have forgotten the laws of your God, I will forget to bless your children.

GW – ⁶ I will destroy my people because they are ignorant. You have refused to learn, so I will refuse to let you be my priests. You have forgotten the teachings of your God, so I will forget your children.

KJV – ⁶ My people are destroyed for lack of knowledge: because thou hast rejected knowledge, I will also reject thee, that thou shalt be no priest to me: seeing thou hast forgotten the law of thy God, I will also forget thy children.

Matthew 19:7-8 –Pg 21

NLT – ⁷ "Then why did Moses say in the law that a man could give his wife a written notice of divorce and send her away?" they asked. 8 Jesus replied, "Moses permitted divorce only as a concession to your hard hearts, but it was not what God had originally intended.

GW – ⁷ The Pharisees asked him, "Why, then, did Moses order a man to give his wife a written notice to divorce her?" ⁸ Jesus answered them, "Moses allowed you to divorce your wives because you're heartless. It was never this way in the beginning.

KJV –⁷ They say unto him, Why did Moses then command to give a writing of divorcement, and to put her away? ⁸ He saith unto them, Moses because of the hardness of your hearts suffered you to put away your wives: but from the beginning it was not so.

John 3:14 – Pg 51

NLT – ¹⁴ And as Moses lifted up the bronze snake on a pole in the wilderness, so the Son of Man must be lifted up,

GW – ¹⁴ "As Moses lifted up the snake on a pole in the desert, so the Son of Man must be lifted up.

KJV –¹⁴ And as Moses lifted up the serpent in the wilderness, even so must the Son of man be lifted up:

Matthew 10:5-6 – Pg 55

NLT – ⁵ Jesus sent out the twelve apostles with these instructions: "Don't go to the Gentiles or the Samaritans, ⁶ but only to the people of Israel—God's lost sheep.

GW – ⁵ Jesus sent these twelve out with the following instructions: "Don't go among people who are not Jewish or into any Samaritan city. ⁶ Instead, go to the lost sheep of the nation of Israel.

KJV –⁵ These twelve Jesus sent forth, and commanded them, saying, Go not into the way of the Gentiles, and into any city of the Samaritans enter ye not: ⁶ But go rather to the lost sheep of the house of Israel.

Revelation 12:9 – Pg 63

NLT – ⁹ This great dragon—the ancient serpent called the devil, or Satan, the one deceiving the whole world—was thrown down to the earth with all his angels.

GW – ⁹ The huge serpent was thrown down. That ancient snake, named Devil and Satan, the deceiver of the whole world, was thrown down to earth. Its angels were thrown down with it.

KJV –⁹ And the great dragon was cast out, that old serpent, called the Devil, and Satan, which deceiveth the whole world: he was cast out into the earth, and his angels were cast out with him.

Matthew 7:24-26 – Pg 65

NLT – ²⁴ "Anyone who listens to my teaching and follows it is wise, like a person who builds a house on solid rock. ²⁵ Though the rain comes in torrents and the floodwaters rise and the winds beat against that house, it won't collapse because it is built on bedrock. ²⁶ But anyone who hears my teaching and doesn't obey it is foolish, like a person who builds a house on sand.

GW – ²⁴ "Therefore, everyone who hears what I say and obeys it will be like a wise person who built a house on rock. ²⁵ Rain poured, and floods came. Winds blew and beat against that house. But it did not collapse, because its foundation was on rock. ²⁶ "Everyone who hears what I say but doesn't obey it will be like a foolish person who built a house on sand.

KJV –²⁴ Therefore whosoever heareth these sayings of mine, and doeth them, I will liken him unto a wise man, which built his house upon a rock: ²⁵ And the rain descended, and the floods came, and the winds blew, and beat upon that house; and it fell not: for it was founded upon a rock. ²⁶ And every one that heareth these sayings of mine, and doeth them not, shall be likened unto a foolish man, which built his house upon the sand:

Matthew 19:5- Pg 65

NLT – ⁵ And he said, "'This explains why a man leaves his father and mother and is joined to his wife, and the two are united into one.'
GW – ⁵ and that he said, 'That's why a man will leave his father and mother and will remain united with his wife, and the two will be one'?
KJV –⁵ And said, For this cause shall a man leave father and mother, and shall cleave to his wife: and they twain shall be one flesh?

NLT (New Living Translation)
GW (God's Word Translation)
KJV (Kings James Version)

Made in the USA
Columbia, SC
11 February 2019